NEW ED...ES SOLD!

Th...te
Gu...er

Parts 1, 2 & 3

About This Book

Welcome to **The Complete Guitar Player** - the best-selling guitar course designed to teach you how to play the guitar by using easy-to-follow explanations, illustrations and tips, while learning all your favourite songs!

This long established course has been fully revised. Well-known songs and clearly presented, illustrated text make learning easy and playing fun. The material is carefully graded, with simplified notation used in the earlier stages, and can be followed by even very young guitarists.

The Complete Guitar Player can be used successfully whether you're learning at home, with a teacher, or in a classroom. Each song is shown either on a single page, or on facing pages, so you won't need to turn the pages while playing.

As you progress through the three parts of the course, you are shown how to build on the styles and techniques that you are learning. More music theory is introduced and illustrated with many new songs and popular classical pieces, which are melodic and easy to master.

The final stage of the course moves smoothly from intermediate through to more advanced playing. Techniques such as the hammer-on and pull-off are explained, and more complicated rhythms introduced. You'll be shown how to extend your repertoire, use musical notation and how to play in many different styles... and become a **Complete Guitar Player**.

Remember to practise a little each day. But above all, have fun!

Introduction

Russ Shipton

Part 1

Exclusive distributors:
Music Sales Limited
8/9 Frith Street, London W1D 3JB, England.
Music Sales Pty Limited
120 Rothschild Avenue, Rosebery, NSW 2018, Austr

Order No. OP48197
This book © Copyright 2001 Omnibus Press
(A Division of Book Sales Limited)

Written and arranged by Russ Shipton.
Edited by Sorcha Armstrong.
Cover and book design by Michael Bell Design.
Cover and guitar photography by George Taylor.
Guitars supplied by Rhodes Music.
Artist photographs courtesy of
    London Features International, Retna and
    The Lebrecht Collection.
Music processed by Paul Ewers Music Design.
Printed in the United Kingdom.

CD programmed by John Moores.
All guitars by Arthur Dick.
Engineered by Kester Sims.

Your guarantee of quality:
As publishers, we strive to produce every book
to the highest commercial standards.
The music has been freshly engraved and the book
has carefully designed to minimise awkward page tu
and to make playing from it a real pleasure.
Particular care has been given to specifying
acid-free, neutral-sized paper made from pulps
which have not been elemental chlorine bleached.
This pulp is from farmed sustainable forests and
was produced with special regard for the environmen
Throughout, the printing and binding have been
planned to ensure a sturdy, attractive publication
which should give years of enjoyment.
If your copy fails to meet our high standards, please
inform us and we will gladly replace it.

Music Sales' complete catalogue describes
thousands of titles and is available in full colour
sections by subject, direct from Music Sales Limited.
Please state your areas of interest and send a
cheque/postal order for £1.50 for postage to:
Music Sales Limited, Newmarket Road, Bury St. Edmu
Suffolk IP33 3YB.

www.omnibuspress.co

NEW EDITION! OVER 1 MILLION COPIES SOLD!

The Complete Guitar Player

by Russ Shipton

Part 1

Useful Information

Strumming Style

Bass-Strum Style

Arpeggio Style

Lyrics

Songs & Music

The Capo

Your Guitar

Machine Heads
(Tuning Pegs)

Nut

Frets

Fingerboard

Neck

Sound Hole

Table (Face)

Bridge Saddle

Body

Bridge

The Capo

It would be very useful for you to have a 'capo'.
This device helps you to make the level of playing
(the pitch of the notes) suit the range of the voice.
The capo is illustrated and discussed on the
pull-out chart.

The Flatpick

You might prefer to use a flatpick for the
strumming and bass-strum styles as it will save your
fingernails from wearing down and help you to
produce more volume.

Holding Your Guitar

When playing modern guitar styles, this is the
way you can hold your guitar:

The Right Hand

When strumming with the fingers, hold them
close together. For picking styles, put the wrist out
to the front slightly and keep the thumb a little to
the left of the fingers. The index, middle and ring
fingers are held over the three treble strings.

When strumming with a flatpick, hold it firmly
between the thumb and side of the index finger.

The Left Hand

The fingertips press the strings down.
The palm of the hand should be kept clear of the
neck. The thumb should be behind the 1st and
2nd fingers, midway on the neck for a good grip
and free movement.

General

The crook of your arm should grip the 'corner'
of the guitar body. Then your right hand should
fall over the rear half of the sound hole. Try not to
have a cramped position. Both hands should be
clear of the guitar, giving the fingers room to move.

Tuning Your Guitar

Check the tuning of your guitar every time you pick it up. What you play will sound better and the tuning process will help to develop your 'ear' or sense of pitch.

The easiest way to tune your strings is to match them with the guitar strings played on the CD (if you have bought the book & CD version). Many players use electronic tuners which check the pitch of each string. Another possibility is to use 'relative tuning' after one string has been tuned correctly.

Relative Tuning

Check the pitch of the 1st string by comparing it to an electronic keyboard or tuning fork. The open 1st string (i.e. with no finger on it) should be an **e** note. If you have an **a** tuning fork, the 5th fret note should match the pitch produced by the fork. Tighten or loosen the string gradually until the pitch of the string is correct. When the 1st string is the right pitch, follow these steps to tune the other strings in relation to it:

Tune your 2nd string to the 1st string. Put your left hand finger on the 5th fret of the 2nd string and play the note with the right hand or flatpick. Now play the open 1st string. These two notes should be the same. Tighten the 2nd string if it's too low in pitch and loosen it if it's too high.

Tune your 3rd string to the open 2nd string. This time press the 4th fret of the 3rd string down and sound the note. It should be the same as the open 2nd string. *Tune the 4th to the open 3rd, the 5th to the open 4th and the 6th to the open 5th* by comparing the 5th fret note on the lower string to the pitch of the string above.

The diagram below shows the first five frets of the guitar fingerboard and where you should put your finger for tuning each string relative to the next:

Strings

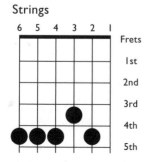

Your First Chord

Hold your guitar as shown on the previous page, and finger an **A** chord. The diagram below is a chord 'window', showing the end of the fingerboard (imagine the guitar neck pointing to the sky). Thus the strings are going down the page. The numbers in circles tell you which finger to use. Your index finger is 1, middle 2, ring 3 and little one 4.

The picture below shows you how the chord should look. All 3 fingers are on the same fret (the second fret) so twist your hand to the left slightly. Try to have a slight gap between the neck of the guitar and your hand.

A Chord

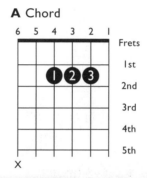

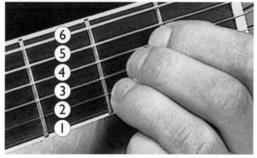

Press all 3 fingers down firmly, with your thumb about midway on the back of the neck, and play each string (start with the 5th string, A) with your right hand thumb, or flatpick. The 5th and 1st strings are played 'open' i.e. with no finger on them. The X underneath the 6th string means 'don't play this string'. Play each string slowly, one by one, and move your finger or hand to stop any buzzing. Got a 'clean' sound now? Good.

Let's have a look at two more chords so you can play your first song...

Mull Of Kintyre

Wings

WarmUp

1 + 2 = 3 Magic Chords

Hundreds of songs can be played with just three chords. The two other chords that are usually found with the **A** chord are the **D** and **E** chords...

D Chord

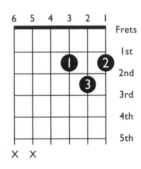

E Chord

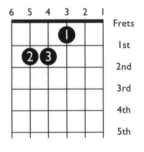

Hold each chord as shown and play the strings one at a time (for the **D** chord, don't play the 6th or 5th strings). If you get buzzing noises, here are some possible reasons:

You're not pressing down on the strings hard enough. Your nails may be too long.

The back of another finger is getting in the way. Or your hand is touching the 1st string. Try to adjust your fingers and hand so the top of the finger is more vertical (not so flat).

Your finger is not close enough to the metal strip (fretwire) in front of it. The further from the strip your finger is, the harder you'll have to press to avoid buzzing. With some chords, like **A**, you can't always get every finger close to it, but try to get as close as you can.

When you can play all three chords cleanly, you're ready to try your first strum.

Your First Strum

Finger an **A** chord. Holding them together, brush down with the backs of your right hand fingers across the strings from 5th to 1st (bass to treble). Extend the fingers as your hand moves downwards. Now try this simple rhythm:

3/4 Rhythm

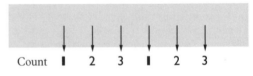

The arrows indicate downward strums. Count each group '1 2 3', as shown, keeping the beats evenly spaced. The first strum of three is stressed by playing it louder. This creates the 3/4 rhythm.

Now try the same rhythm pattern with the **D** and **E** chords. Keep the pace quite slow for the moment. Finally, try to change chords with the left hand while keeping the rhythm steady with the right. Once you can do this, have a go at the accompaniment on the next page.

Don't try to go too fast, otherwise you'll have to stop to change chords, and it might be hard to change the habit.

Strumming Style

A D E = Chords
↓ = Strum down

Accompaniment: 3/4 Rhythm

Chorus

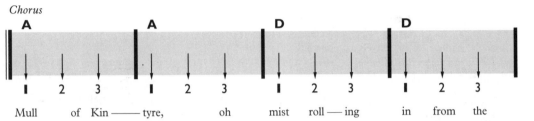

A			A			D			D		
1	2	3	1	2	3	1	2	3	1	2	3
Mull	of	Kin——tyre,		oh		mist	roll——ing		in	from	the

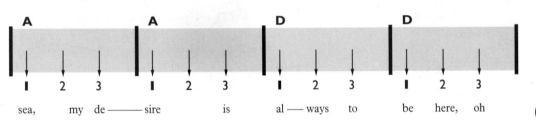

A			A			D			D		
1	2	3	1	2	3	1	2	3	1	2	3
sea,	my	de——sire		is		al——ways	to		be	here,	oh

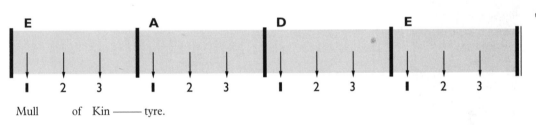

E			A			D			E		
1	2	3	1	2	3	1	2	3	1	2	3
Mull	of	Kin——tyre.									

Strumming Style

(Notes)

Bar Lines: *Separate the groups of 3 strums. The 1st beat/strum in each bar is the heavy one.*

Length Of Strums: *Don't try to hit all the strings on every strum. Perhaps you can start by hitting 5 or 6 strings for the heavy strum, and 3 or 4 strings on the others.*

Using The Flatpick: *Instead of using your right hand fingers, you might prefer using a flatpick. Keep it angled slightly so it glides across the strings. Whether you use your fingers or flatpick, don't hit the strings too hard!*

Singing: *When you're able to change chords smoothly and play through the accompaniment at a moderate pace, try singing the chorus words as shown. The first melody note is the 2nd fret of the 4th string.*

Verse: *The verse chords are shown with the other lyrics on page 37.*

Words & Music by Paul McCartney & Denny Laine
© Copyright 1977 MPL Communications Limited, 1 Soho Square, London W1.
All Rights Reserved. International Copyright Secured.

The Times They Are A-Changin'

Bob Dylan

WarmUp

Strumming Style

Chord Changing

The **A**, **D** & **E** chords are used again for this song. Can you remember them without looking at the diagrams? The sooner you remember the chords, the quicker you'll progress.

If you're having trouble changing chords, try putting your 1st finger down first, and the others just after. In no time you'll find you can put them all down together!

Take all accompaniments slowly to start with, and then you won't have to stop or slow down to get into the next chord position. When you can play the whole song slowly, try speeding up to the correct tempo.

Singing

Most people find singing a little strange at first, but almost everybody is able to pitch their voice correctly to make a reasonable sound. So persevere, even if you feel a little awkward now. I've made the timing of the singing a little easier to follow than the original songs in many cases. When you're in complete control of the playing side of things, time the words as you feel fit. It would help your general progress if you committed the 1st verse (and chorus where appropriate) to memory.

Upstrums

Now you've got the simple 3/4 strum pattern mastered, let's complicate things with upstrums. As your fingers come up to be ready for the next downstrum, they can strike some treble strings on the way. These upstrums are off the beat and not so 'important' as the downstrums, so they can be hit more lightly. Only two or three treble strings need be played.

If you want to use a flatpick, turn your wrist to angle the pick the other way for the upstrums:

Hold an **A** chord and play a downstrum followed by an upstrum:

Now play several in a row:

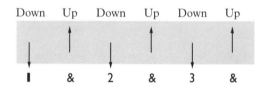

Make sure the upstrums are exactly halfway between the downstrums. Patterns often involve just one or two upstrums. In 'The Times They Are A-Changin', the first pattern has one upstrum. Count it: 1 2 & 3. The other pattern has two upstrums and is counted: 1 & 2 & 3. Play the accompaniment with just the first pattern, then with just the second pattern.

Finally, alternate the patterns as shown. It's a lot to remember, especially while singing, but it's worth the effort!

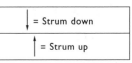

Accompaniment: 3/4 Rhythm

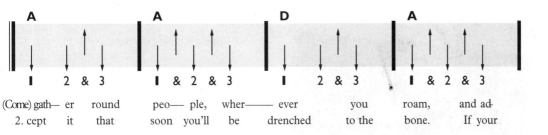

(Come) gath— er round   peo— ple, wher——ever   you   roam,   and ad-
2. cept   it   that   soon you'll be   drenched   to the   bone.   If your

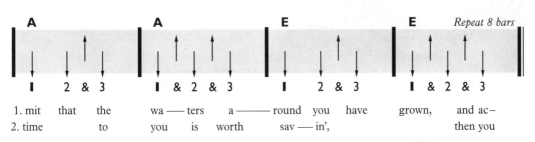

1. mit   that   the   wa — ters   a ——round you   have   grown,   and ac–
2. time   to   you   is   worth   sav — in',   then you

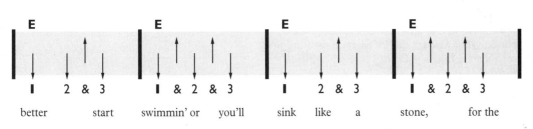

better   start   swimmin' or   you'll   sink   like   a   stone,   for the

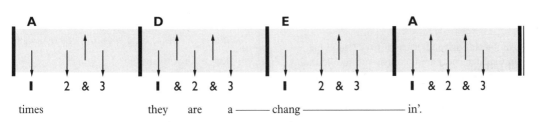

times   they   are   a ——— chang ——————— in'.

Strumming Style

Ⓝ **Notes**

Speed: *Play the accompaniment slowly at first. Keep the beats evenly spaced and the rhythm as steady as possible. Repeat the first 8 bars with the second line of lyrics.*

Extra Bars: *As Bob Dylan often does, add one or more bars of **A** at the end of the sequence, before singing the second verse.*

Melody Notes: *Singing this song is easy at the start - the 2nd fret note of the 3rd string is used for every syllable of 'Come gather round people'.*

Words & Music by Bob Dylan
© Copyright 1963 & 1964 Warner Brothers Music, USA.
All Rights Reserved. International Copyright Secured.

Candle In The Wind

Elton John & Bernie Taupin

WarmUp

Strumming Style

What's A Chord?

We're staying with the same three chords for this and the next song, so you'll get to know them perfectly. But what are they? Well, they consist of several notes that sound pretty good when played together.

Count the notes in each chord - you should find 6 for **E**, 5 for **A**, and 4 for **D**. But though in a way you're right, some notes are similar enough to be given the same name (these are said to be octaves of each other). So basically these chords have three notes in them, though some are repeated.

All the chords you'll learn in Part 1 (and many in the later ones) are the most 'normal' sounding chords. Some are called 'major' chords; like the ones you've learned so far.

Below I've shown another rhythm for you to try, and now you know the **A**, **D** and **E** chords quite well, see if you can stop looking at your left hand, even when it changes chords. Then you can concentrate on what your right hand is doing. It's very important to get a steady rhythm. You'll also have time to give some attention to your singing.

Another Rhythm

The most common rhythm in modern music is 4/4. If the first number indicates the number of beats, what do you think the basic strumming pattern for this rhythm will be? Yes, you've guessed it. A heavy strum followed by three lighter ones. Let's try it...

4/4 Rhythm Hold any chord

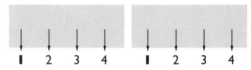

Count **1** 2 3 4, **1** 2 3 4, etc. Stress the first beat strum and follow with three lighter strums. Keep the strums evenly spaced, as before.

Melody Notes

The melody notes are usually the notes that are sung. You could also try playing the single notes while a friend plays the chorus accompaniment as shown. Or you could record yourself playing the chords, then play the melody along with the recording.

String	⌐2nd⌐	⌐ Ist⌐	2nd	⌐ Ist ⌐	⌐2nd⌐
Fret	2 3 0	0 0 2	0	0 0 2	3

And it seems to me you lived your life like a

⌐Ist⌐	3rd ⌐2nd⌐	⌐ Ist ⌐
0 0 0 2	2 2 3	0 0 0 0 2 0

candle in the wind, never knowing who to cling to

⌐ 2nd ⌐	⌐ Ist ⌐
3 2 2 0 0	0 0 2 2 2 4

when the rain set in. And I would have liked to

⌐ Ist ⌐	3rd 2nd 3rd ⌐2nd⌐
4 5 4 4 2 0	2 2 2 2 2 2

have known you, but I was just a kid. Your candle

2nd Ist ⌐2nd⌐	⌐4th⌐ ⌐3rd⌐2nd4th
3 0 2 0 0	2 4 2 2 0 4

burnt out long before your legend ever did.

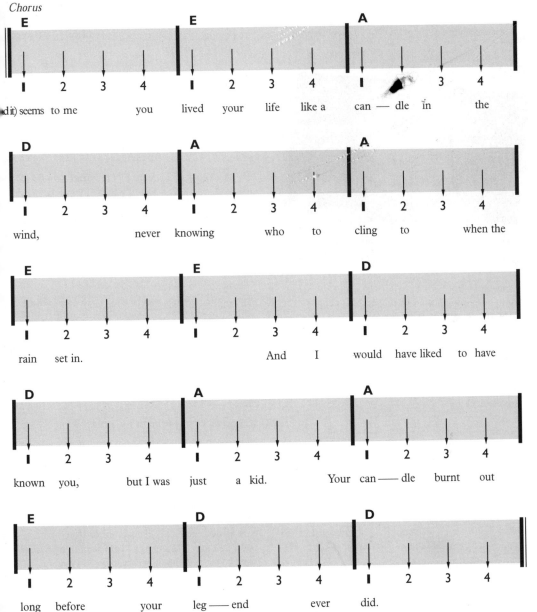

$\downarrow$ = Strum down

Accompaniment: 4/4 Rhythm

Chorus

E	E	A
1 2 3 4	**1** 2 3 4	**1** 2 3 4
dit) seems to me you	lived your life like a	can — dle in the

D	A	A
1 2 3 4	**1** 2 3 4	**1** 2 3 4
wind, never knowing	who to	cling to when the

E	E	D
1 2 3 4	**1** 2 3 4	**1** 2 3 4
rain set in.	And I	would have liked to have

D	A	A
1 2 3 4	**1** 2 3 4	**1** 2 3 4
known you, but I was	just a kid.	Your can — dle burnt out

E	D	D
1 2 3 4	**1** 2 3 4	**1** 2 3 4
long before your	leg — end	ever did.

Strumming Style

(Notes)

Singing: *Sing 'And it' before starting the accompaniment for the chorus shown above.*

Verse: *The verse chords are shown with the other lyrics on page 38.*

Ending: *The last chord shown is a* **D**, *but you can add a bar of* **A** *and a bar of* **E** *before singing the verse. Finish the song with an* **A** *chord strum after the two bars of* **D**.

Words & Music by Elton John & Bernie Taupin
© Copyright 1973 Dick James Music Limited. Universal /Dick James Music Limited, 77 Fulham Palace Road, London W6.
All Rights Reserved. International Copyright Secured.

Blowin' In The Wind

Bob Dylan

Upstrums

As we did with the 3/4 rhythm, let's add some upstrums to the simple 4/4 pattern, and make things sound a bit more interesting. Finger an **E** chord and try these patterns:

4/4 Rhythm

Count **⏐** & 2 & 3 & 4

Count **⏐** 2 & 3 & 4

Accompaniment: 4/4 Rhythm

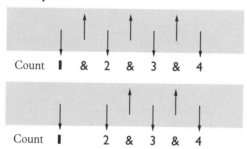

Verse

A					**D**						**A**				
⏐	2	&	3	&	4	**⏐**	2	&	3	&	4	**⏐**	2	&	3	&	4

1. How	man —— y	roads		must	a	man		walk
2. how	man —— y	seas		must	the	white		dove
3. how	man —— y	times		must	the	cannon		balls

Notice the extra upstrum in the last bar of both verse and chorus. Don't forget to keep a steady rhythm (and slow to start with), with each downstrum equally spaced whether or not there's an upstrum before or after it.

Melody Notes

Singing the first note of a song is not always easy. Find out which note in the chord is the one you sing for the first word (occasionally it's not a note in the chord that I show first but that doesn't matter). It makes for a much stronger beginning if you know exactly what note you're about to sing!

The first note of 'Blowin' In The Wind' (for 'How') is found on the 2nd fret of the 4th string, or the open 1st string for high voices. As a change to playing the normal accompaniment, try playing the melody while a friend plays the chorus. Here are the notes of the chorus, with the string and fret shown, as before:

String		2nd			3rd		2nd		3rd
Fret	3	3	3	2	0	2	2	2 2 0	2

The answer, my friend, is blowin' in the wind

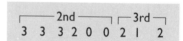

		2nd				3rd	
3	3	3	2	0	0	2 1	2

The answer is blowin' in the wind.

Lyrics

In most cases the words of the 1st verse are shown beneath the notation. When parts of the song are very similar, later words are put under the same bars of notation. This gives you less to remember. Soon you'll be using many slight variations to make your guitar accompaniments more interesting.

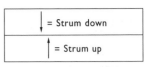

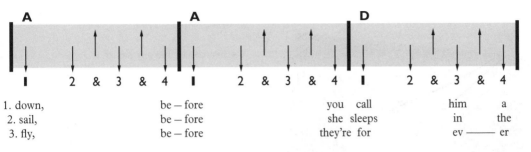

1. down,   be — fore   you   call   him   a
2. sail,   be — fore   she sleeps   in   the
3. fly,   be — fore   they're for   ev ——————— er

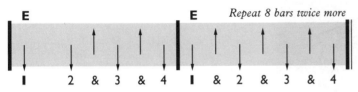

1. man?
2. sand?
3. banned?   Yes'n
                                  The

Chorus

Strumming Style

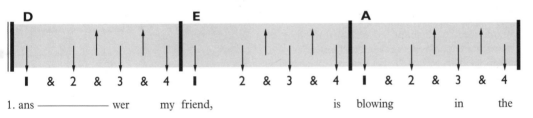

1. ans ——————————— wer   my friend,   is   blowing   in   the

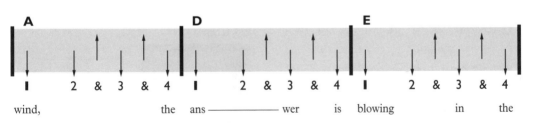

wind,   the   ans ——————————— wer   is   blowing   in   the

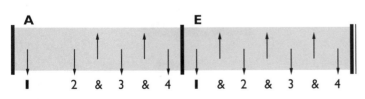

wind.

Words & Music by Bob Dylan
© Copyright 1962 Warner Brothers Music, USA. © Copyright renewed 1990 SPECIAL RIDER MUSIC.
This arrangement © Copyright 2000 SPECIAL RIDER MUSIC.
All Rights Reserved. International Copyright Secured.

Hey Jude

The Beatles

Strumming Style

Downstrums Between Beats

Another kind of rhythmic feel is created when *downstrums* are played between beats instead of upstrums. This sort of rhythm pattern often suits slow ballads:

4/4 Rhythm Hold any chord

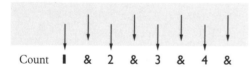

Count   I   &   2   &   3   &   4   &

Make the downstrums between the beats shorter than those on the beats, across two or three lower strings. Stress the 1st beat strum more than the others, but to get the correct rhythmic feel you must do a full strum on each beat and *stress all the beats reasonably heavily*. This will produce more of a 'plodding' rhythm. The strums between beats must again be played exactly halfway between.

As with the previous strum patterns, some strums between beats can be removed to create different patterns. Try this variation:

4/4 Rhythm Hold any chord

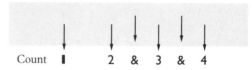

Count   I   2   &   3   &   4

E7 Chord

So far you've used the **A**, **D** and **E** chords only. These are simple major chords involving three notes. When **A** is the main chord, you could try using an **E7** (**E** seventh) chord instead of **E**. This creates a stronger 'pull' back to the **A** chord and provides more variety. 7th chords have four notes, one more than the ordinary major chord. Here are two easy ways of holding an **E7** chord:

E7 Chord

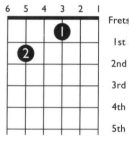

E7 Chord

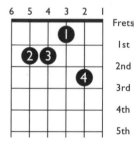

The extra note is an octave higher in the second **E7** shown. Try both shapes in the accompaniment for 'Hey Jude'.

Accompaniment: 4/4 Rhythm

Strumming Style

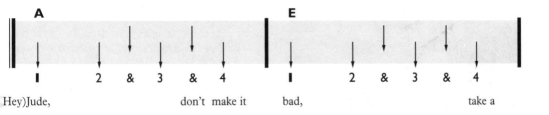

A

| I | 2 | & | 3 | & | 4 |

Hey)Jude,   don't make it

E

| I | 2 | & | 3 | & | 4 |

bad,   take a

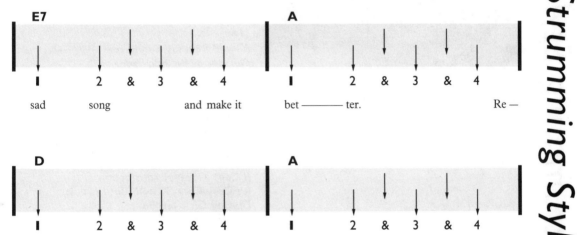

E7

| I | 2 | & | 3 | & | 4 |

sad   song   and make it

A

| I | 2 | & | 3 | & | 4 |

bet —— ter.   Re —

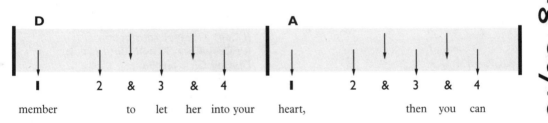

D

| I | 2 | & | 3 | & | 4 |

member   to   let   her   into your

A

| I | 2 | & | 3 | & | 4 |

heart,   then   you   can

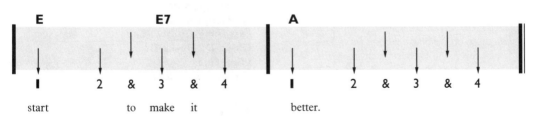

E   E7

| I | 2 | & | 3 | & | 4 |

start   to   make   it

A

| I | 2 | & | 3 | & | 4 |

better.

Notes

Middle Section: *The chords for the middle section of 'Hey Jude' are given with the other lyrics on page 39.*

Melody: *The first two notes of the tune are the open 1st string and 2nd fret of the 2nd string.*

Mid-Bar Chord Change: *Notice the chord change in the seventh bar. Add your little finger or remove the 3rd finger on the 3rd beat of the bar.*

Summary

Strum Patterns

Here are the 3/4 and 4/4 strum patterns you've already seen, plus a few more...

3/4 Rhythm

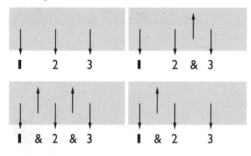

4/4 Rhythm

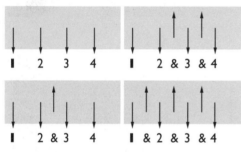

4/4 Rhythm *(with downstrums between beats)*

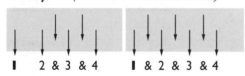

Play each of the patterns over and over until you can play them smoothly at different speeds. Experiment with putting different patterns together in an accompaniment.

You could also create some patterns of your own by varying the number of offbeat strums. An upstrum might be added at the end of a pattern when the same chord is used for the following bar.

With an upstroke at the end, the second 3/4 pattern would be counted: **1** 2 & 3 &. Then you'd go straight into the first beat or downstrum of the next bar. Putting an upstroke at the end of the second 4/4 pattern, it would be counted: **1** 2 & 3 & 4 &.

Other Songs

Here is a list of other songs that you can play with *just three chords*:

3/4
A Hard Rain's A-Gonna Fall
The Happy Birthday Song
Lucille
The Wild Rover
There Goes My Everything
Irene Goodnight
Amazing Grace

4/4
(I Can't Get No) Satisfaction
It's Only Rock 'N Roll (But I Like It)
Leaving On A Jet Plane
C'mon Everybody
Three Steps To Heaven
The Sloop John B.
Rave On
Heartbeat
Bad Moon Rising
Save The Last Dance For Me
Last Thing On My Mind
Ob-La-Di, Ob-La-Da
I Feel Fine
The Ballad Of John And Yoko

4/4 *(with downstrums between beats)*
Let It Be
Get Back
I Still Haven't Found What I'm Looking For
Brimful Of Asha
Father And Son
Knockin' On Heaven's Door
The Joker

How To Do It

The bass-strum style is halfway between strumming and finger-picking. Your thumb strikes individual strings, and the fingers brush across the treble strings. Normally the strums are shorter than in ordinary strumming.

Let's have a look at the simple 3/4 and 4/4 patterns...

3/4 Rhythm Finger an **A** Chord

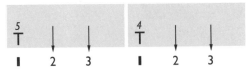

4/4 Rhythm Finger an **E** Chord

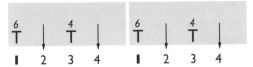

As you've guessed, the 'T's mean the thumb strikes. The number on top of the T means the string your thumb has to hit. In the patterns shown above, the thumb strike replaces a downstrum on the first beat of every bar in the 3/4 rhythm. In the 4/4 bars, two downstrums are replaced by thumb strikes: the first and the third.

Count the bars as usual, keeping a steady rhythm. Don't move your right hand too much, or your thumb won't be in the right position for the next bass string strike.

Using A Flatpick

Many players use a flatpick for the bass-strum style instead of thumb and fingers. If you used a pick for the strumming style, you could also try it for this style too. Strike the individual string that is indicated above the 'T' in the notation.

Use a downward motion and keep the right hand quite close to the strings to help you hit the correct bass string.

Right, you're ready for some more great songs!

Simple 4/4 Pattern Sequence
Finger an **E** chord

Thumb strikes 6th string

Strum down

Thumb strikes 4th string

Strum down

Bass-Strum Style

Catch The Wind

Donovan

Bass-Strum Style

Two New Chords

When a song starts and ends with an **A** chord, it will have been played 'in the key of **A**'. The two other chords usually found with the **A** chord are the **D** and **E** chords, as you've seen. When a song starts and ends with the **D** chord, the key will be **D**, and the other two chords generally found with the **D** chord will be the **A** and **G** chords.

You already know the **A** chord, but quite often, when moving to the **D** chord, the **A** seventh (**A7** for short) will be used. So let's have a look at the **A7** and the **G** chords.

A7 Chord

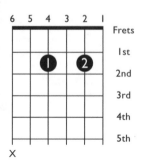

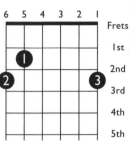

G Chord

The **A7** can also be fingered with the 2nd and 3rd fingers. If you find it easier, for the moment you could use the 4th finger instead of the 3rd for the **G** chord. Keep the left hand thumb on the middle of the back of the neck.

Upstrokes

The accompaniment involves two alternating bass-strum patterns, one with no upstrums, and the other with a single upstrum. To start with, you could use just the first pattern throughout, then the second pattern throughout, then finally play both as shown.

Melody Notes

Here are the notes of 'Catch The Wind' to help you sing the melody correctly. You could also play them on the guitar along with the accompaniment (played on CD or by a friend).

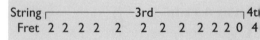

String					3rd							4t
Fret	2	2	2	2	2	2	2	2	2	2	2 0	4

In the chilly hours and minutes of uncertainty

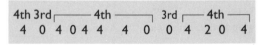

4th	3rd			4th			3rd		4th		
4	0	4	0	4	4	4	0	0	4	2 0	4

I want to be in the warm hold of your lovin' mind.

The second half of the verse has a similar melody, but with a **D** note to finish.

$\overset{4}{T}$ = Thumb plays 4th string
↓ = Strum down
↑ = Strum up

Accompaniment: 3/4 Rhythm

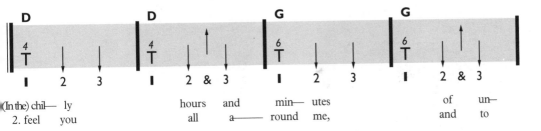

(In the) chil— ly   hours   and   min— utes   of   un—

2. feel   you   all   a—— round   me,   and   to

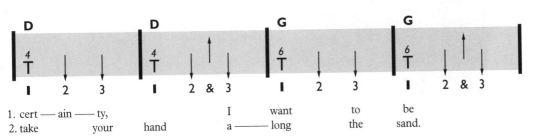

1. cert —— ain —— ty,   I   want   to   be

2. take   your   hand   a —— long   the   sand.

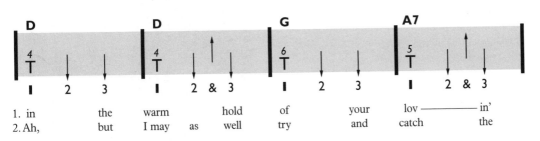

1. in   the   warm   hold   of   your   lov ———— in'

2. Ah,   but   I may   as   well   try   and   catch   the

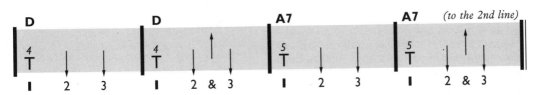

(to the 2nd line)

1. mind,

2. wind!

Ⓝⓞⓣⓔⓢ **Speed:** _As usual play the accompaniment slowly at first. When you can remember the sequence, try singing the top line of words. The 2nd half of the verse has the same chord sequence._

Bass Notes: _When two bars in a row involve the same chord, you can strike a different bass string. Try striking the 5th string in bars 2, 4, 6 & 10 for a more varied sound._

Words & Music by Donovan Leitch
© Copyright 1965 Donovan (Music) Limited, 8-14 Verulam Street, London WC1.
All Rights Reserved. International Copyright Secured.

Mr. Tambourine Man

Bob Dylan

Bass-Strum Style

'Clean Playing'

This is a reminder to those of you who may be blindly (or is it deafly?) bashing away, without really listening to the sort of sounds you and your guitar are producing. Can you answer 'Yes' to these three questions?

Are you tuning your guitar every time you pick it up?
If it's not in very good tune, however well you follow my directions, the overall sound won't be very nice to listen to.

Are you pressing down hard enough on the strings?
However well you do with your rhythm, it's your left hand that determines the quality of the sound that comes out. Try to practise a little each day and the ends of your fingers will harden up. Then you'll find it easier to press down.

Are your left hand finger nails very short?
Cut them regularly and that'll help you press down on the strings properly. Don't let your fingers get too far from the metal strip (fret wire) either, and that'll help you get a 'clean' sound. If you concentrate for a couple of weeks on producing pure sounds, with little or no buzzing noises, after that you'll soon do it automatically. It's a good time to get rid of any bad habits!

Using The Capo

In my 'useful information' notes at the start of the book, I mentioned the capo. If you find the melody of a song too low for you to sing comfortably, try using your capo.

In the picture below, a **D** chord (shape) is fingered, but with a capo placed on the third fret. The capo effectively shortens the neck of the guitar and increases the pitch of all the strings by the same amount. This means that the capo can be treated as the end of the neck (i.e. as the 'nut') and the same shapes can be fingered.

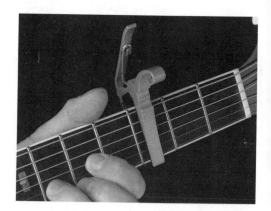

Bass Notes

For the **D** chord (and sometimes the **G**), I've given the 3rd string as a 'bass string' strike. Though the 6th, 5th and 4th strings are generally considered to be the bass strings and the other three the treble, in this and other picking styles the 3rd is often picked out by the thumb or pick.

After striking the 3rd string you can still hit it along with the others for the strums following.

Accompaniment: 4/4 Rhythm

Chorus

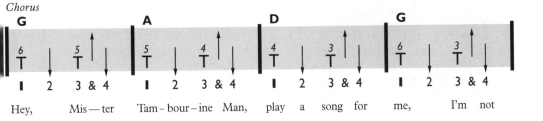

Hey,   Mis — ter   Tam - bour – ine Man,   play   a   song   for   me,   I'm   not

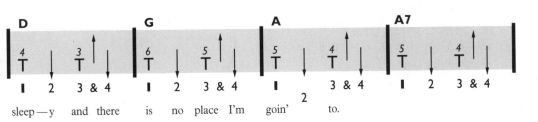

sleep — y   and there   is   no   place I'm   goin'   to.

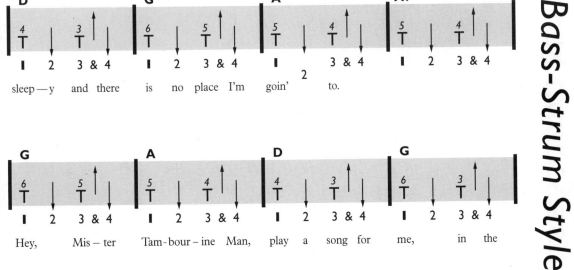

Hey,   Mis – ter   Tam - bour – ine   Man,   play   a   song   for   me,   in   the

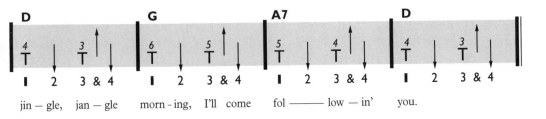

jin — gle,   jan — gle   morn — ing,   I'll   come   fol ——— low — in'   you.

Bass-Strum Style

Notes

Melody: *To help with your singing, the first notes of the chorus can be found on the 3rd & 2nd frets of the 2nd string.*

Chords: *Notice that the chorus begins with the* **G** *chord (as does the verse). As Bob Dylan does, you can add one or two* **D** *bars before starting the verse. The verse lyrics appear on page 40.*

Me And Bobby McGee

Kris Kristofferson

Another Pattern

We're returning to the key of **A** for this great Kris Kristofferson song. I've added another upstrum and some bass variations, but the first note in each bar is always the usual one i.e. 5th for **A**, 6th for **E** and 4th for **D**.

Upstrum Before Chord Change

An upstrum on the offbeat may come just before a chord change. Although the sound is often muffled because the left hand is actually moving when the right hand strikes, the rhythm is kept going.

Don't worry about getting clear notes on strums immediately before a chord change, just make sure your left hand is in the new chord position for the next beat.

Bass-Strum Style

Accompaniment: 4/4 Rhythm

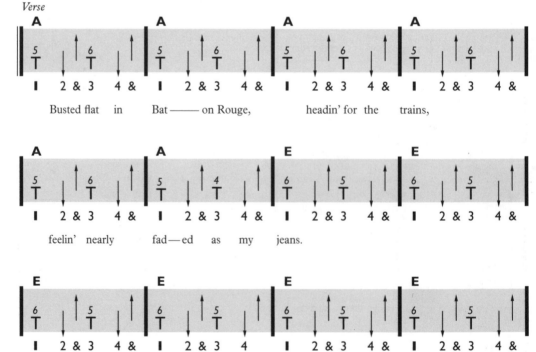

Verse

Busted flat in Bat——on Rouge, headin' for the trains,

feelin' nearly fad—ed as my jeans.

Bobby thumbed a dies—el down, just before it rained,

$\frac{5}{T}$ = Thumb plays 5th string

↓ = Strum down

↑ = Strum up

Bass-Strum Style

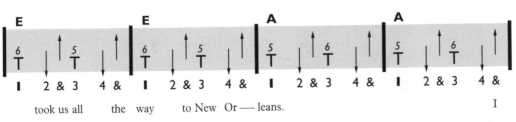

took us all   the way   to New Or — leans.   I

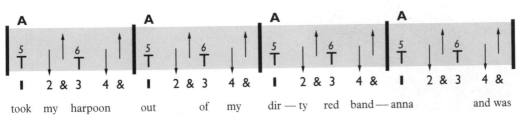

took   my   harpoon   out   of   my   dir — ty   red   band — anna   and was

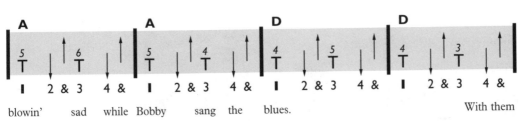

blowin'   sad   while Bobby   sang   the   blues.   With them

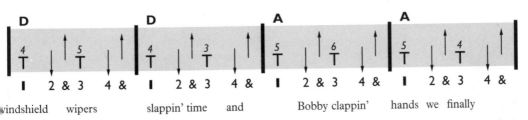

windshield   wipers   slappin' time   and   Bobby clappin'   hands   we   finally

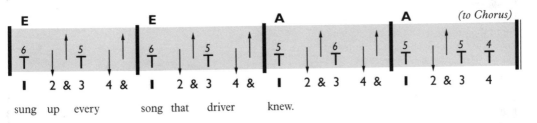

(to Chorus)

sung   up   every   song   that   driver   knew.

(Notes)

The Starting Note *for singing this song can be found on the 2nd fret of the 4th string.*

The Chorus *is given, with chords, on page 41.*

Words & Music by Kris Kristofferson & Fred Foster
© Copyright 1969 Combine Music Corporation, USA. EMI Songs Limited, 127 Charing Cross Road, London WC2.
All Rights Reserved. International Copyright Secured.

25

Love Is All Around

Wet Wet Wet

You could use one of three possible variations: change the bass note for beat 3; pick out the same bass note on beat 3 as beat 1; or pick out a bass note on beat 1 but not on beat 3. You could even use a strumming pattern without single notes to vary the sound and give the middle section a 'heavier' feel.

Minor Chords

So far you've learnt four major chords and two 7th chords. Another kind of chord is often found in accompaniments, the *minor* chord. In the key of **D** you may well come across the **Em** chord, as in 'Love Is All Around'.

Em (E Minor) Chord

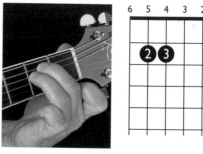

Downstrums Between Beats

Like the strumming style, slower songs should sometimes be played with downstrums between beats, instead of upstrums. Here is the same type of pattern that you used for 'Hey Jude', except two single bass notes are struck on the 1st & 3rd beats:

4/4 Rhythm Finger a **D** Chord

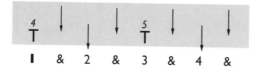

The downstrums between beats should again be played across two or three lower strings. Count the pattern as shown, but the tempo for 'Love Is All Around' should be a little faster than that for 'Hey Jude'. Use the pick if it feels more comfortable for you than thumb and fingers.

Different Patterns

The verse of 'Love Is All Around' has a chord change in each bar, but the pattern still involves single notes on the 1st and 3rd beats. The chorus (shown on page 41) has one chord per bar.

If you hold an **E** chord and remove your 1st finger, it becomes an **Em**. You'll notice that this slight change produces a 'sad' kind of sound, whereas major chords are more upbeat. You can also hold this shape with the 1st & 2nd fingers.

Melody Notes

To help your singing, here's the melody of the first line of lyrics (the second line is the same):

String	5th	4th			5th	
Fret	2	4 4 2	0	2	2	

I feel it in my fingers,

3rd	4th				
0 0	4 2	0	4		

I feel it in my toes.

$\overset{4}{T}$ = Thumb plays 4th string

$\downarrow$ = Strum down

Accompaniment: 4/4 Rhythm

Verse

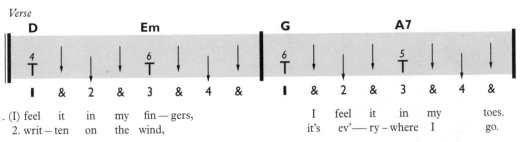

1. (I) feel it in my fin — gers,
2. writ – ten on the wind,

I feel it in my toes.
it's ev'— ry – where I go.

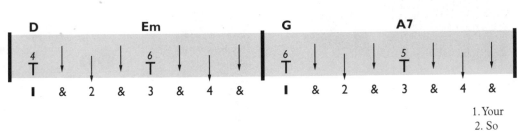

1. Your
2. So

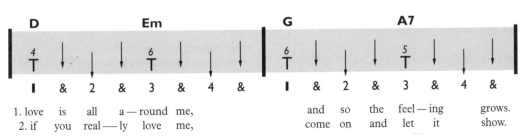

1. love is all a — round me,
2. if you real — ly love me,

and so the feel — ing grows.
come on and let it show.

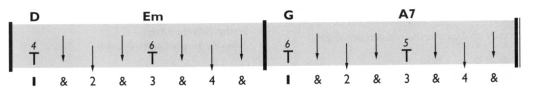

2. It's

Bass-Strum Style

Words & Music by Reg Presley
© Copyright 1967 Dick James Music Limited. Universal/Dick James Music Limited, 77 Fulham Palace Road, London W6.
All Rights Reserved. International Copyright Secured.

Summary

Now go back to the songs you've played in this section (and then to some of those listed on this page) and try using different patterns.

Bass-Strum Style

Bass-Strum Patterns

A variety of bass-strum patterns are shown below, including the ones you've used for accompaniments already:

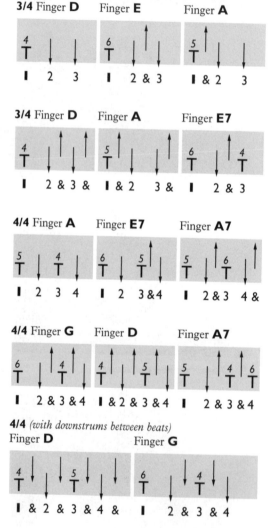

3/4 Finger **D**   Finger **E**   Finger **A**

3/4 Finger **D**   Finger **A**   Finger **E7**

4/4 Finger **A**   Finger **E7**   Finger **A7**

4/4 Finger **G**   Finger **D**   Finger **A7**

4/4 *(with downstrums between beats)*
Finger **D**   Finger **G**

Removing or adding upstrums can change the feel of the rhythm. Experiment with some variations of your own.

Bass-Pluck Style

A very similar style to the bass-strum style is the 'bass-pluck' style, which also uses the bass string strikes as the key feature of the accompaniment. Instead of the strums, you pick all three treble strings together (pluck means an upward pick) with the first three right hand fingers.

The two simple 3/4 and 4/4 patterns work well for this style, and will sound fine for many light and traditional songs.

Other Songs

Here are a few suggestions for songs to play in the bass-strum style, all of which can be played with simple chords:

3/4
Masters Of War
On Top Of Old Smokey
My Bonnie
Liverpool Lou
In Dublin's Fair City
With God On Our Side

4/4
Wild Wood
Ruby Don't Take Your Love To Town
I Walk The Line
This Land Is Your Land
I'm The Urban Spaceman
Colours
The Universal Soldier
Hello Marylou
You're My Best Friend
This Train
It Doesn't Matter Anymore
Rocky Mountain High
Take Me Home Country Roads

4/4 *(with downstrums between beats)*
Hey Joe
Heart Of Gold
Baby I Love Your Way
The Border Song
Mighty Quinn
Oh Danny Boy
A Groovy Kind Of Love

How To Do It

This style of playing involves picking out individual chord notes one after the other by the thumb and three right hand fingers. Try this bar in the 3/4 rhythm:

3/4 Rhythm Finger an **A** Chord

5 T					
	i	*m*	*r*	*m*	*i*
I	&	2	&	3	&

The three right hand fingers are indicated by 'i', 'm' & 'r' (index, middle and ring fingers).

Here and in the accompaniments that follow, the *index finger always plucks the 3rd string*, the *middle finger always strikes the 2nd string*, and the *ring finger always strikes the 1st string*.

As before, the large 'T' and the small number on top of it stand for the thumb strike and which string to play.

Hold your three fingers over the top three treble strings and pluck them in the order shown, after the thumb strike. Don't get the fingers caught under the strings by playing too hard. Make the finger plucks gentle and flowing. Count the pattern as shown. Stress the beat notes more and keep the rhythm steady. Now try a 4/4 pattern:

4/4 Rhythm Finger a **G** Chord

6 T				4 T			
	i	*m*	*r*		*i*	*m*	*r*
I	&	2	&	3	&	4	&

Because the arpeggio style is flowing and continuous, your left hand needs to move quickly to the new position when there is a chord change. If an open bass string note starts the new chord it will be easier, but if it's a fretted note (as in a **G** chord), you must make sure the finger is on the (6th) string in time.

When you can play the 3/4 and 4/4 arpeggio patterns smoothly, you're ready to enjoy some more great songs...

Simple 4/4 Pattern Sequence
Finger an **A** Chord

Thumb strikes 5th string

1st Finger strikes 3rd string

2nd Finger strikes 2nd string

3rd Finger strikes 1st string

Repeat the above sequence to complete a full 4/4 pattern, but start the second half with a 4th string thumb strike.

Arpeggio Style

Scarborough Fair

Traditional, arranged by Russ Shipton

Arpeggio Style

Minor Keys

Most songs are written in a major key, and the ones you've played so far have all been major. This means the main chord (and the one that the accompaniment will end on) is a major one. Some songs are written in a minor key, where the main chord is minor.

The next song is given in the key of **A** minor. The **Am** chord is shown below, along with another popular chord, **C** major:

Am (A Minor) Chord

6 5 4 3 2 1	Frets
	1st
	2nd
	3rd
	4th
	5th

X

C Chord

6 5 4 3 2 1	Frets
	1st
	2nd
	3rd
	4th
	5th

X

Although the fingering is quite different between an **A** and an **Am**, notice that there is still just one note changed, and by just one fret.

Helpful Hints

Notice that the bass note changes when another bar of the same chord follows. To start with, you could play the same note again to make things easier. Play the thumb strikes quite hard and make the treble notes softer - your fingers should just brush over the strings.

Near the end of the accompaniment there's a bar of **Em** with just one strum. This helps to create more variety. Play the strum right across all the strings, deliberately and not too fast. Then rest for two beats while singing 'love of'. After that you're back to the usual pattern for two bars of **Am** before beginning the next verse.

Don't forget to experiment with the capo to match your vocal range.

Melody Notes

Here are the melody notes for you to check that you've got the tune right, and for playing along with the accompaniment given. Also why not try using a strumming pattern against the arpeggio? They should sound pretty good together.

String	⌐3rd⌐	⌐1st⌐	⌐2nd⌐	3rd
Fret	2 2	0 0 0	0 1	0 2

Are you going to Scarborough Fair?

⌐1st⌐	2nd 1st
0 3 5 3 0 2	3 0

Parsley, sage, rosemary and thyme.

⌐1st⌐	⌐2nd⌐3rd
5 5 5 3 0 0 0	3 1 0 2 0

Remember me to the one who lives there,

3rd 1st ⌐2nd⌐	⌐3rd⌐
2 0 3 1 0	2 0 2

she once was a true love of mine.

Accompaniment: 3/4 Rhythm

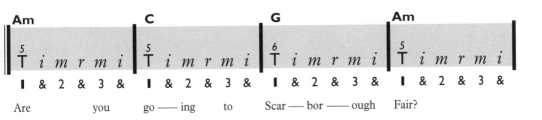

Am	C	G	Am
$\frac{5}{\mathsf{T}}$ i m r m i	$\frac{5}{\mathsf{T}}$ i m r m i	$\frac{6}{\mathsf{T}}$ i m r m i	$\frac{5}{\mathsf{T}}$ i m r m i
I & 2 & 3 &	I & 2 & 3 &	I & 2 & 3 &	I & 2 & 3 &

Are   you   go —— ing   to   Scar — bor —— ough   Fair?

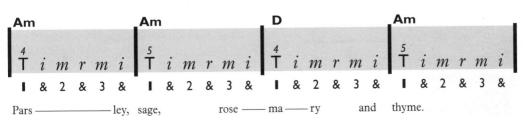

Am	Am	D	Am
$\frac{4}{\mathsf{T}}$ i m r m i	$\frac{5}{\mathsf{T}}$ i m r m i	$\frac{4}{\mathsf{T}}$ i m r m i	$\frac{5}{\mathsf{T}}$ i m r m i
I & 2 & 3 &	I & 2 & 3 &	I & 2 & 3 &	I & 2 & 3 &

Pars ———— ley,   sage,   rose — ma — ry   and   thyme.

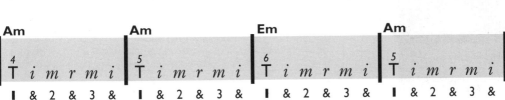

Am	Am	Em	Am
$\frac{4}{\mathsf{T}}$ i m r m i	$\frac{5}{\mathsf{T}}$ i m r m i	$\frac{6}{\mathsf{T}}$ i m r m i	$\frac{5}{\mathsf{T}}$ i m r m i
I & 2 & 3 &	I & 2 & 3 &	I & 2 & 3 &	I & 2 & 3 &

Re — mem — ber   me   to the   one   who   .   lives

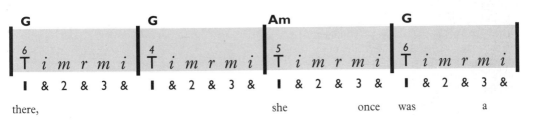

G	G	Am	G
$\frac{6}{\mathsf{T}}$ i m r m i	$\frac{4}{\mathsf{T}}$ i m r m i	$\frac{5}{\mathsf{T}}$ i m r m i	$\frac{6}{\mathsf{T}}$ i m r m i
I & 2 & 3 &	I & 2 & 3 &	I & 2 & 3 &	I & 2 & 3 &

there,   she   once   was   a

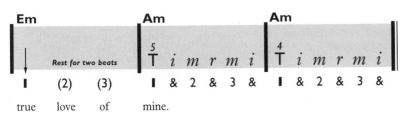

Em	Am	Am
↓ **Rest for two beats**	$\frac{5}{\mathsf{T}}$ i m r m i	$\frac{4}{\mathsf{T}}$ i m r m i
I (2) (3)	I & 2 & 3 &	I & 2 & 3 &

true   love   of   mine.

Arpeggio Style

Traditional
© Copyright 2000 Dorsey Brothers Music Limited, 8-9 Frith Street, London W1.
All Rights Reserved. International Copyright Secured.

Why Worry

Dire Straits

Arpeggio Style

Another Key

You've used two major keys so far, **A** & **D**. This next accompaniment is written in another popular guitar key, the key of **E** major. The three main chords in this key are **E**, **A** & **B**, but because the **B** chord is hard to finger many guitarists prefer to use the **B7** chord instead:

B7 Chord

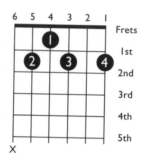

All four fingers are used for the **B7**. The 2nd string is played open but the 6th string shouldn't be sounded.

Alternative Patterns

When you've mastered the accompaniment on the next page, try changing the order of the treble strings and maybe mixing the patterns up for variety and different effects. Here are two possibilities, try inventing some of your own:

4/4 Rhythm Finger an **E** Chord

⑥ T	r	m	i	④ T	r	m	i
I	&	2	&	3	&	4	&

4/4 Rhythm Finger a **B7** Chord

⑤ T	i	r	m	④ T	i	r	m
I	&	2	&	3	&	4	&

Remember that the index finger always strikes the 3rd string, the middle finger the 2nd string and the 3rd finger the top string.

Alternative Styles

Many songs sound better if they're played in a particular style. Often that will mean the way they were arranged by the original writer. Sometimes though, it might be worth experimenting with different styles to see what they sound like for the same song.

In the classroom, different groups can play alternative styles at the same time. At home you could do the same thing by playing along with a recording or a friend.

Melody Notes

The chorus of 'Why Worry' is given on the next page. Here are the melody notes:

String	⌐3rd⌐	4th	⌐	3rd	⌐	4th	⌐	3rd
Fret	2 I	2	2	2	2 4	4	2 4	I

Why worry, there should be laughter after pain,

	⌐	3rd	⌐	⌐4th⌐	3rd
2	2	2	I	4	2 4 I

there should be sunshine after rain.

	⌐	3rd	⌐⌐	4th ⌐	3rd
2	2	2	I 4	2	4 I

These things have always been the same,

4th⌐	3rd⌐	4th	⌐3rd⌐	4th
4 2	I I	2	2 I I	2

so why worry now, why worry now?

T	= Thumb
i	= Index finger
m	= Middle finger
r	= Ring finger

Accompaniment: 4/4 Rhythm

Chorus

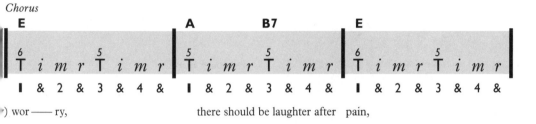

>) wor —— ry,   there should be laughter after   pain,

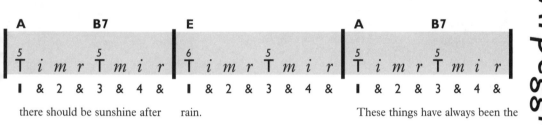

> there should be sunshine after   rain.   These things have always been the

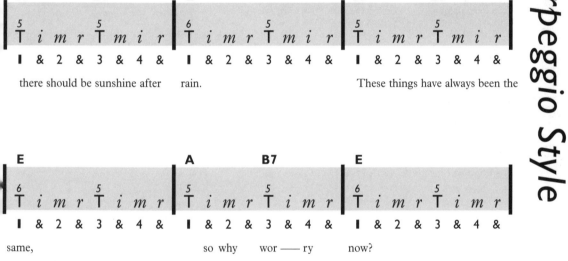

> same,   so why   wor —— ry   now?

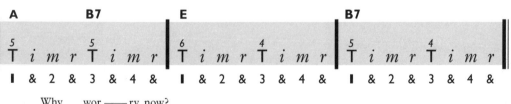

> Why   wor ——ry now?

Arpeggio Style

Notes

Verses: *The verses of 'Why Worry' are given on page 42.*

Words & Music by Mark Knopfler
© *Copyright 1985 Chariscourt Limited.*
All Rights Reserved. International Copyright Secured.

Wonderful Tonight

Eric Clapton

Arpeggio Style

The Key Of G Major

Another popular guitar key is **G** Major.
This is the key that Eric Clapton uses to play the song himself. The main chords are **G**, **C** & **D**.
The **Em** chord often occurs in the key of **G** Major (as well as **D** Major, where you saw it).

Melody Notes

Here are the notes to help you sing the verse of 'Wonderful Tonight':

String	4th	┌2nd┐	3rd	2nd	3rd	┌2nd┐		
Fret	0	0 1	0	2	3	0 1	1	

It's late in the evening, she's wond'rin

┌2nd┐	┌3rd┐	4th	┌2nd┐	3rd 2nd
0 0	2 2	0	0 1 0	2 3

what clothes to wear. She puts on her make-up,

3rd	┌2nd┐	┌3rd┐
0 0	1 0 0	2 2

and brushes her long, blonde hair.

┌1st┐	2nd 3rd	┌2nd┐	3rd
0 0	0 3 2	0 0 0	3 0

And then she asks me, "Do I look all right?"

┌3rd┐	┌2nd┐	┌3rd┐	4th 3rd
0 2 0	1 1 0	2 2 0	0 0

And I say "Yes, you look wonderful tonight."

The middle section chords are shown with all the song lyrics on page 42.

More Patterns

As well as switching the order of the treble strings, the rhythmic feel can be altered by changing the number and position of the thumb strikes. You could try this pattern for 'Wonderful Tonight' instead of the one shown:

4/4 Rhythm Finger a **G** Chord

6						5	
T	i	m	r	m	i	T	i
1	&	2	&	3	&	4	&

Accompaniment: 4/4 Rhythm

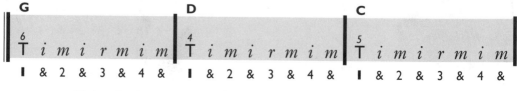

Verse																							
G								**D**								**C**							
6								4								5							
T	i	m	i	r	m	i	m	T	i	m	i	r	m	i	m	T	i	m	i	r	m	i	m
1	&	2	&	3	&	4	&	1	&	2	&	3	&	4	&	1	&	2	&	3	&	4	&

It's late in the eve — ning,   she's wondering what

D

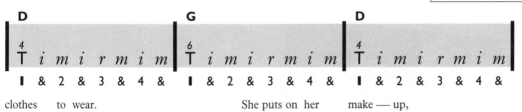

4

T i m i r m i m

1 & 2 & 3 & 4 &

G

6

T i m i r m i m

1 & 2 & 3 & 4 &

D

4

T i m i r m i m

1 & 2 & 3 & 4 &

clothes   to wear.   She puts on her   make — up,

C

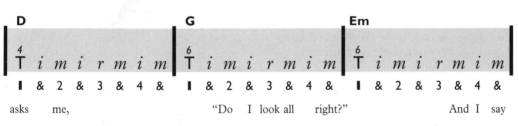

5

T i m i r m i m

1 & 2 & 3 & 4 &

D

4

T i m i r m i m

1 & 2 & 3 & 4 &

C

5

T i m i r m i m

1 & 2 & 3 & 4 &

and brushes her   long,   blonde   hair.   And then she

D

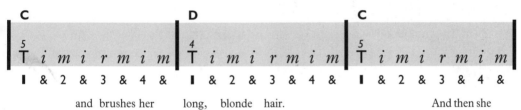

4

T i m i r m i m

1 & 2 & 3 & 4 &

G

6

T i m i r m i m

1 & 2 & 3 & 4 &

Em

6

T i m i r m i m

1 & 2 & 3 & 4 &

asks   me,   "Do I look all   right?"   And I say

C

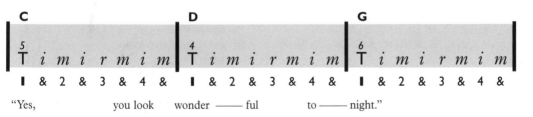

5

T i m i r m i m

1 & 2 & 3 & 4 &

D

4

T i m i r m i m

1 & 2 & 3 & 4 &

G

6

T i m i r m i m

1 & 2 & 3 & 4 &

"Yes,   you look   wonder —— ful   to —— night."

D

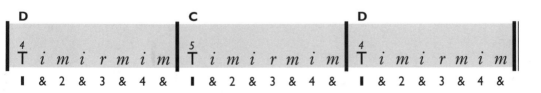

4

T i m i r m i m

1 & 2 & 3 & 4 &

C

5

T i m i r m i m

1 & 2 & 3 & 4 &

D

4

T i m i r m i m

1 & 2 & 3 & 4 &

Arpeggio Style

Words & Music by Eric Clapton

Summary

Arpeggio Style

Arpeggio Patterns

A variety of arpeggio patterns are shown below, including those you've already used in this section:

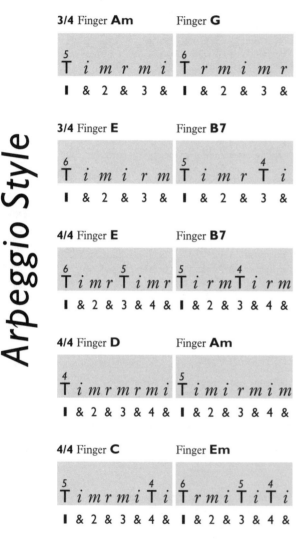

3/4 Finger **Am**

T i m r m i
1 & 2 & 3 &

Finger **G**

T r m i m r
1 & 2 & 3 &

3/4 Finger **E**

T i m i r m
1 & 2 & 3 &

Finger **B7**

T i m r T i
1 & 2 & 3 &

4/4 Finger **E**

T i m r T i m r
1 & 2 & 3 & 4 &

Finger **B7**

T i r m T i r m
1 & 2 & 3 & 4 &

4/4 Finger **D**

T i m r m r m i
1 & 2 & 3 & 4 &

Finger **Am**

T i m i r m i m
1 & 2 & 3 & 4 &

4/4 Finger **C**

T i m r m i T i
1 & 2 & 3 & 4 &

Finger **Em**

T r m i T i T i
1 & 2 & 3 & 4 &

Changing the order of the fingers and the number of bass strikes can alter the feel of the rhythm. Experiment with some variations of your own.

Now go back to the songs you've played in this section (and then to some of those listed on this page) and try using different patterns.

Other Songs

Many slower, ballad-type songs are suited to the arpeggio style. You're sure to recognise some of the songs listed below, all of which can be played with simple chords and will sound great with an arpeggio accompaniment.

3/4
Bird On A Wire
Lavender's Blue
Around The World
When Two Worlds Collide
Mistletoe And Wine
Sisters Of Mercy
Joan Of Arc
Amazing Grace

4/4
The Rose
Turn, Turn, Turn
Wild Mountain Thyme
Where Have All The Flowers Gone
Hey, That's No Way To Say Goodbye
From Both Sides Now
The Sound Of Silence
The Leaving Of Liverpool
Carrickfergus
English Country Garden
A Little Peace
Green Green Grass Of Home
A Groovy Kind Of Love

Mull Of Kintyre

Verse 1

A	A	A	A

Far have I travelled and much have I seen

D	D	A	A

Dark distant mountains with valleys of green

A	A	A	A

Past painted deserts, the sunset's on fire

D	D	E	A A

As he carries me home to the Mull of Kintyre.

Chorus

Mull of Kintyre, oh mist rolling in from the sea
My desire is always to be here, oh Mull of Kintyre.

Verse 2

Sweep through the heather like deer in the glen
Oh carry me back to the days I knew then
Nights when we sang like a heavenly choir
Of the life and the times of the Mull of Kintyre

Verse 3

Smiles in the sunshine and tears in the rain
Still take me back where my memories remain
Flickering embers grow higher and higher
As they carry me back to the Mull of Kintyre.

The Times They Are A-Changin'

Verse 1

Come gather round people, wherever you roam
And admit that the waters around you have grown
And accept it that soon you'll be drenched to the bone
If your time to you is worth savin'
Then you'd better start swimmin' or you'll sink
    like a stone
For the times they are a-changin'.

Verse 2

Come writers and critics who prophesise with your pen
And keep your eyes wide, the chance won't come again
And don't speak too soon for the wheel's still in spin
And there's no tellin' who that it's namin'
For the loser now will be later to win
For the times they are a-changin'.

Verse 3

Come senators, congressmen, please heed the call
Don't stand in the doorway, don't block up the hall
For he that gets hurt will be he who has stalled
There's a battle outside ragin'
It'll soon shake your windows and rattle your walls
For the times they are a-changin'.

Verse 4

Come mothers and fathers throughout the land
And don't criticise what you can't understand
Your sons and your daughters are beyond
    your command
Your old road is rapidly agin'
Please get out of the new one if you can't lend
    your hand
For the times they are a-changin'.

Verse 5

The line it is drawn, the curse it is cast
The slow one now will later be fast
As the present now will later be past
The order is rapidly fadin'
And the first one now will later be last
For the times they are a-changin'.

Lyrics

Candle In The Wind

Verse 1

  A   **A**   **D**
Goodbye Norma Jean, though I never knew you
  D
   at all
              A   **A**
You had the grace to hold yourself, while those
       D   **D**
   around you crawled
            A   **A**
They crawled out of the woodwork, and they
    D   **D**
   whispered into your brain
            A   **A**
They set you on a treadmill and they made you
         D
   change your name.

Chorus
And it seems to me you lived your life like a candle
   in the wind
Never knowing who to cling to when the rain set in
And I would have liked to have known you, but
   I was just a kid
Your candle burnt out long before your legend ever did.

Verse 2
Loneliness was tough, the toughest role you
   ever played
Hollywood created a superstar and pain was the
   price you paid
Even when you died the press still hounded you
All the papers had to say was that Marilyn was found in
   the nude.

Verse 3
Goodbye Norma Jean, though I never knew
   you at all
You had the grace to hold yourself while those
   around you crawled
Goodbye Norma Jean, from the young man in
   the twenty-second row
Who sees you as something more than sexual,
   more than just our Marilyn Monroe.

Blowin' In The Wind

Verse 1
How many roads must a man walk down
Before you call him a man?
How many seas must the white dove sail
Before she sleeps in the sand?
Yes'n how many times must the cannon balls fly
Before they're forever banned?

Chorus
The answer, my friend, is blowin' in the wind
The answer is blowin' in the wind.

Verse 2
Yes'n how many years can a mountain exist
Before it is washed to the sea?
Yes'n how many years can some people exist
Before they're allowed to be free?
Yes'n how many times can a man turn his head
And pretend that he just doesn't see?

Verse 3
Yes'n how many times must a man look up
Before he can see the sky?
Yes'n how many ears must one man have
Before he can hear people cry?
Yes'n how many deaths will it take till he knows
That too many people have died?

Lyrics

Hey Jude

Verse 1
Hey Jude, don't make it bad
Take a sad song and make it better
Remember to let her into your heart
Then you can start to make it better.

Verse 2
Hey Jude, don't be afraid
You were made to go out and get her
The minute you let her under your skin
Then you begin to make it better.

Middle Section

A (A7)   **D**   **D**
And any time you feel the pain, hey Jude, refrain
             E   **A**   **A (A7)**
Don't carry the world upon your shoulders
                     D   **D**
For well you know that it's a fool who plays it cool
             E   **A**
By making his world a little colder
        A   **E**   **E (E7)**
Na na na na-na, na na na na.

Verse 3
Hey Jude, don't let me down
You have found her, now go and get her
Remember to let her into your heart
Then you can start to make it better.

Middle Section 2
So let it out and let it in
Hey Jude, begin
You're waiting for someone to perform with
And don't you know that it's just you
Hey Jude, you'll do
The movement you need is on your shoulders.
Na na na na-na, na na na na.

Verse 4
Hey Jude, don't make it bad
Take a sad song and make it better
Remember to let her under your skin
Then you'll begin to make it better.

Better, better, better, better, better, oh...

Na, na, na, na na na na... na na na na...
Hey Jude.

Catch The Wind

Verse 1
In the chilly hours and minutes of uncertainty
I want to be in the warm hold of your lovin' mind
To feel you all around me and to take your hand
   along the sand
Ah, but I may as well try and catch the wind.

Verse 2
When sundown pales the sky
I want to hide a while behind your smile
And everywhere I'd look your eyes I'd find
For me to love you now would be the sweetest thing
   it would make me sing
Ah, but I may as well try and catch the wind.

Verse 3
When rain has hung the leaves with tears
I want you near to kill my fears
To help me to leave all my blues behind
For standin' in your heart is where I want to be and
   I long to be
Ah, but I may as well try and catch the wind.

Mr. Tambourine Man

Verse 1

<pre>
            G   A   D
Though I know that evening's empire has returned
            G
   into sand
D   G   D   G
Vanished from my hand, left me blindly here to stand
              A   A
But still not sleepin'
       G   A   D   G
My weariness amazes me, I'm branded on my feet
     D   G   D   G
I have no one to meet, and the ancient, empty street's
                    A   A
   too dead for dreamin.'
</pre>

Chorus

Hey, Mister Tambourine Man, play a song for me
I'm not sleepy and there is no place I'm goin' to
Hey, Mister Tambourine Man, play a song for me
In the jingle, jangle morning I'll come followin' you.

Verse 2

Take me on a trip upon your magic, swirlin' ship
My senses have been stripped, my hands can't
  feel to grip
My toes too numb to step, wait only for my boot
  heels to be wanderin'
I'm ready to go anywhere, I'm ready for to fade
Into my own parade, cast your dancin' spell my way
I promise to go under it.

Verse 3

Though you might hear laughin', spinnin', swingin'
Madly across the sun, it's not aimed at anyone
It's just escapin' on the run, and but for the sky
  there are no fences facin'
And if you hear vague traces of skippin' reels of rhyme
To your tambourine in time, it's just a ragged
  clown behind
I wouldn't pay it any mind, it's just a shadow
  you're seein' that he's chasin'.

Verse 4

Then take me disappearin' through the smoke
  rings of my mind
Down the foggy ruins of time, far past the frozen leaves
The haunted, frightened trees, out to the windy beach
Far from the twisted reach of crazy sorrow
Yes, to dance beneath the diamond sky with one
  hand wavin' free
Silhouetted by the sea, circled by the circus sands
With all memory and fate driven deep beneath
  the waves
Let me forget about today until tomorrow.

Me And Bobby McGee

Verse 1

Busted flat in Baton Rouge, headin' for the trains
Feelin' nearly faded as my jeans
Bobby thumbed a diesel down, just before it rained
Took us all the way to New Orleans
I pulled my harpoon out of my dirty red bandanna
And was blowin' sad while Bobby sang the blues
With them windshield wipers slappin' time
And Bobby clappin' hands
We finally sang up every song that driver knew.

Chorus 1

| D | D | A | A |

Freedom's just another word for nothin' left to lose

| E | E | A | A(A7) |

And nothin' ain't worth nothin', but it's free

| D | D | A |

Feelin' good was easy, Lord, when Bobby sang the blues

| E | E | E E |

Feelin' good was good enough for me

| E (E7) | E (E7) | A | A |

Good enough for me and Bobby McGee.

Verse 2

From the coalmines of Kentucky, to the California sun
Bobby shared the secrets of my soul
Standin' right beside me through everything I done
And every night she kept me from the cold
Then somewhere near Salinas, Lord, I let her slip away
Lookin' for the home I hoped she'd find
Well, I'd trade all my tomorrows for a single yesterday
Holdin' Bobby's body next to mine.

Love Is All Around

Verse 1

I feel it in my fingers, I feel it in my toes
Your love is all around me, and so the feeling grows
It's written on the wind, it's everywhere I go
So if you really love me, come on and let it show.

Chorus

| G | Em |

You know I love you, I always will

| G | D |

My mind's made up by the way that I feel

| G | Em |

There's no beginning, there'll be no end

| Em | A |

'Cause on my love you can depend.

Verse 2

I see your face before me, as I lay on my bed
I kinda get to thinkin' of all the things you said
You gave your promise to me, and I gave mine to you
I need someone beside me in everything I do.

Scarborough Fair

Verse 1

Are you goin' to Scarborough Fair
Parsley, sage, rosemary and thyme
Remember me to one who lives there
She once was a true love of mine.

Verse 2

Tell her to make me a cambric shirt
Parsley, sage, rosemary and thyme
Without any seam or needle work
Then she'll be a true love of mine.

Verse 3

Tell her to find me an acre of land
Parsley, sage, rosemary and thyme
Between the salt water and the sea strand
Then she'll be a true love of mine.

Verse 4

Tell her to plough it with a sickle of leather
Parsley, sage, rosemary and thyme
And bind it all in a bunch of heather
Then she'll be a true love of mine.

Lyrics

Lyrics

Why Worry

Verse 1

E B7   **E B7**
Baby, I see this world has made you sad
                  E   A
Some people can be bad
            (F♯)   **B7 B7**
The things they do, the things they say
      E B7   **E   B7**
But baby, I'll wipe away those bitter tears
                    E   A
I'll chase away those restless fears
         (F♯)   **B7 B7**
That turn your blue skies into grey.

Chorus
Why worry, there should be laughter after pain
There should be sunshine after rain
These things have always been the same
So why worry now, why worry now?

Verse 2
Baby, when I get down I turn to you
And you make sense of what I do
I know it isn't hard to say
But baby, just when this world seems mean and cold
Our love comes shining red and gold
And all the rest is by the way.

Wonderful Tonight

Verse 1
It's late in the evening, she's wonderin' what
   clothes to wear
She puts on her make-up and brushes her long,
   blonde hair
And then she asks me, "Do I look all right?"
And I say, "Yes, you look wonderful tonight."

Verse 2
We go to a party, and everyone turns to see
This beautiful lady, who's walking around with me
And then she asks me, "Do you feel all right?"
And I say, "Yes, I feel wonderful tonight."

Middle Section
       C   **D**   **G**   **Em**
I feel wonderful because I see the love light in your eyes
       C   **D**   **C**   **D**
And the wonder of it all is that you just don't realise
       G
How much I love you.

Verse 3
It's time to go home now, and I've got an achin' head
So I give her the car keys and she helps me to bed
And then I tell her, as I turn out the light
I say, "My darling, you were wonderful tonight."

42

About The Capo

Most acoustic (and many electric) guitarists use this important device. The capo shortens the guitar strings and increases their pitch by the same amount. It can be placed on any fret (just behind the fret wire).

Using The Capo

To be effective, the capo must press all the strings down firmly. The first capo (pictured below) simply clamps across the strings, like a very strong clip or peg. (Here, it is shown on the third fret). The second type (below left) involves a screw which is adjusted so a rubber covered bar is firmly clamped across the strings.

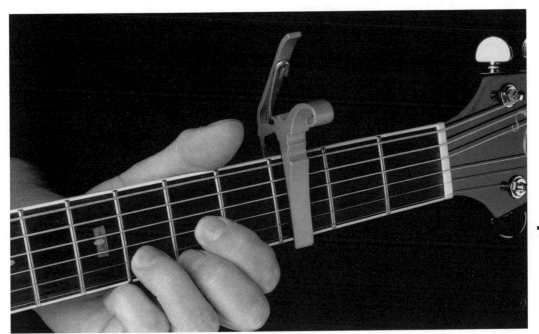

If the pitch of a song doesn't suit your vocal range, the capo can be put somewhere on the neck of the guitar. The position of the capo can be changed until the melody suits your voice.
The same chord shapes can be played as before, but singing will be easier.

One person can play without a capo and use one group of chord shapes, while another can put a capo on and play a different group of chord shapes. They can sound great when played together. Try these two possibilities:-

1st Player (or group)
Chords **A**, **D** and **E** (no capo)
2nd Player (or group)
Chord shapes **D**, **G** and **A** (capo on 7th fret)

1st Player (or group)
Chords **D**, **G** and **A** (no capo)
2nd Player (or group)
Chord shapes **A**, **D** and **E** (capo on 5th fret)

Congratulations!

You've reached the end of Part 1. You're no longer a beginner and the hardest part is over.

Now you know ten chords and various patterns in three quite different right hand styles. This is a good basis for developing a broad ability in guitar playing.

Some of you may have been playing the guitar for a while before using this book, so you may have found it easier than others, but there's always something to gain from any new material. Don't pass over things too quickly. You might not know them as well as you think.

In Parts 2 and 3 of the course I'll gradually explain more music theory, and introduce some classical pieces, so you can see how the different types of music are related.

Those of you who have already studied some music theory should try to tie in your knowledge with what you've been playing on the guitar. A little musical knowledge helps greatly in arranging material quickly and increasing your repertoire.

Before going on to Part 2, try to find some songs that can be played with the chords you know, and experiment with the various right hand styles and patterns. Then I want you to remember the open string notes of the guitar:

e	a	d	g	b	e	Notes
6	5	4	3	2	1	String Numbers

Frets: 1st, 2nd, 3rd, 4th, 5th

Have you committed the open string notes to memory? Good - see you in Part 2 for more great songs and interesting things to learn!

Part 2

The Complete Guitar Player

by Russ Shipton

Part 2

Music Theory

So that you can understand the sheet music of any songs you want to learn and play on your guitar, you must be able to read the melody notes as they're shown on the 'treble clef'. If you don't know, or aren't sure exactly how this standard music notation works, go carefully through this page - it follows simple rules, and is easier than it looks!

The first seven letters of the alphabet are used, but the intervals between them are not the same...

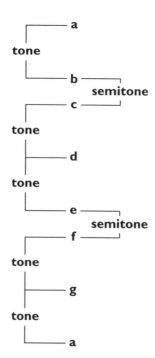

Between the notes **e** and **f** and **b** and **c**, there is no intermediary note. Between the others there is a note that's called 'sharp' or 'flat'. In other words, the note between **a** and **b** may be called **a♯** (sharp) or **b♭** (flat). Can you guess the note between **f** and **g**? Yes, that's right, **f♯** or **g♭**.

Pitch Intervals On The Guitar

Therefore the semitone is the smallest interval of pitch. On the guitar, moving from one fret to the next on the same string is moving a semitone (or from an open note to the 1st fret note of the same string). And moving towards the guitar body the pitch goes higher.

Music Notation

The top line of music in the song sheet or book you buy is the melody. Have a look at the treble clef and where you can find the notes...

This is the symbol for the treble clef.

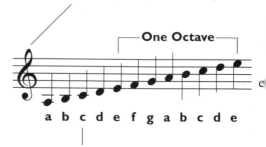

*This is the 'middle **c**' (the **c** note in the middle of the piano). It's the 1st fret, 2nd string on the guitar, but* **guitar music is shown an octave higher than actually played.**

A note is sharpened (raised by a semitone) or flattened (lowered by a semitone) with a sign placed **either** at the start of the line **or** just before it, like this...

As well as the 'pitch' (higher or lower) of the notes, the music notation tells you how long the notes last. Here are the main signs that indicate the length of time each note should last...

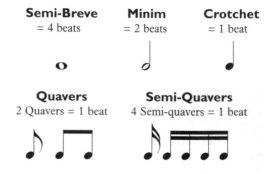

More Ideas

Barre Chords

All guitarists need to learn 'barre' chords. These involve the 1st finger pressing down two or more strings. The **F** chord is an extremely important barre chord shape that requires the 1st finger to go across all six strings:

The F Chord

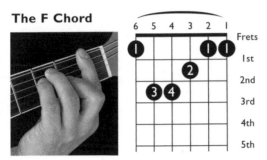

Drop your thumb on the neck and lean towards the end of the guitar. Adjust the 1st finger position to avoid any buzzing. To make it easier to hold the shape you could put your capo on about the 5th fret (and hold the shape on the 6th fret). Some players use their thumb for the 6th string **f** note, with a short barre across the top two or three strings:

The F Chord

The other crucial barre chord you need to learn for this book is **Bm**. Here the barre goes across at the 2nd fret. Use a capo to start with if you need to.

The Bm Chord

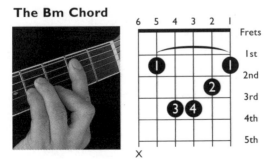

Finding Chord And Melody Notes

Once you've learnt the basic music theory on page 2, you'll soon be able to find and name the notes in the chords you play. You'll also be able to check the melody notes of any song you want to play and sing. For the moment you can try and commit the lower fret notes to memory.

Fill in the other notes on the diagram below. You will then see why the frets indicated are used for tuning your guitar.

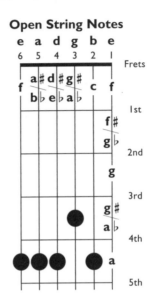

Open String Notes

One piano key to the next along
= 1 semitone

One guitar fret to the next
= 1 semitone

Rhythm Variations

Interesting changes to the strumming style rhythm patterns are introduced in this section. As well as learning how to swing the rhythm, you'll also be using stops and syncopation, i.e. offbeat stress.

Using A Flatpick

If you haven't yet tried using a flatpick, perhaps now is a good time to start. It will save wearing your nails down for the picking styles and allow for a greater volume range. Though it may be difficult at first to try something different, each approach will produce a particular effect and will be well worth mastering.

Yellow Submarine

The Beatles

The swung upstrums are shown visually. It may help you to count the pattern 1, & 2, & 3, & 4, &. Play the pattern over and over, keeping the beats evenly spaced as always. The swing rhythm should feel 'jumpy'.

To start with, play 'Yellow Submarine' with swung upstrums throughout. Then try to vary the number of upstrums as shown in the accompaniment below.

Stress

Though you still emphasise the 1st beat strum, with swing strum accompaniments you should *stress every beat quite heavily*.

Melody

When you're happy with the swing rhythm accompaniment for 'Yellow Submarine', here are the first notes to help you sing the right melody:

b c d b a b g

See if you can find them on the lower frets of the guitar.

The Swing Rhythm

Most of the songs in Part 2 are played with a 'straight' rhythm - i.e. the offbeat strums or notes are played exactly halfway between beats. Some songs, like 'Yellow Submarine', however, must be played with a swing rhythm. Delay the upstrums till just before the following beat:

4/4 Rhythm Hold any chord

Accompaniment: 4/4 Swing Rhythm

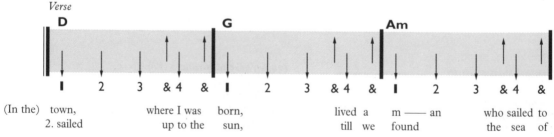

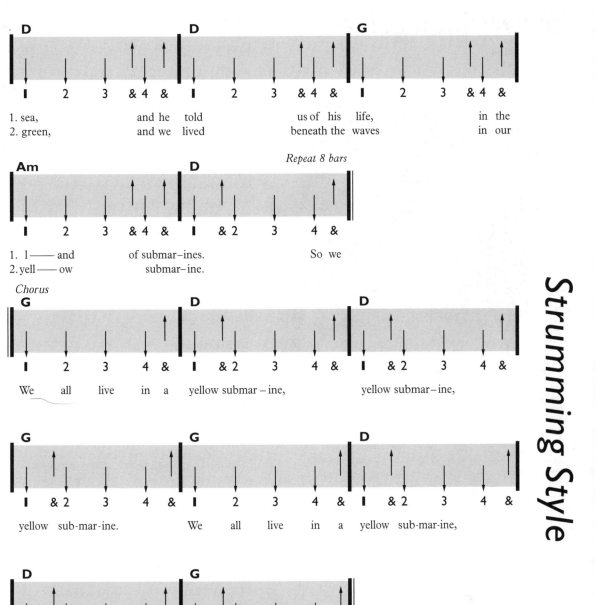

Strumming Style

More Swing Songs

Revolution (The Beatles)
When I'm Sixty-Four (The Beatles)
Girl (The Beatles)
Don't Stop (Fleetwood Mac)

You Ain't Goin' Nowhere (Bob Dylan)
Slip Slidin' Away (Paul Simon)
Song Sung Blue (Neil Diamond)
Summer Holiday (Cliff Richard)
Release Me (Engelbert Humperdink)
Lucille (Kenny Rogers)
When I Need You (Leo Sayer)

American Pie

Don McLean

Strumming Style

New G Chord Fingering

For particular songs the standard chords sometimes need to be altered slightly. The fingering may change or a note or two added. To change quickly and smoothly between the **G** and **C** chords, try this **G** chord fingering:

G Chord

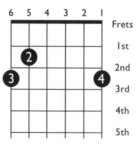

Stops

Continuous down/up strums are used for 'American Pie', apart from the stops on the **Em** chord. These help to vary the sound and improve the song dynamics. Experiment with occasional stops in songs you already know.

Syncopation

So far you've been using stress in the normal way, i.e. on the beats. If you stress an offbeat strum a little tension is created in the rhythm. This is known as 'syncopation'. One way of stressing the offbeat is to come into a chord between beats rather than on a beat. Try changing into the **D** chord *very quickly* in bars 2, 4 & 6 and striking it early, not on the 3rd beat but between beats 2 & 3. This matches the timing of the lyrics:

4/4 Rhythm

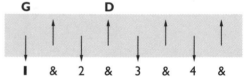

Make the **D** upstrum slightly longer than usual and the downstrum on beat 3 lighter and shorter than usual. The bar is counted the same, but the rhythmic feel is different.

The D Run

An extremely common guitar trick when holding a **D** chord for more than one bar is to remove the 2nd finger or add the 4th finger, or both. Play the last **D** bars normally to start with, then try following the indications above the notation. This produces a treble note run and stresses the offbeat notes. The movement and slight syncopation makes the accompaniment more interesting.

Melody

Here are the first notes of the chorus:

d (low) **d** (high) **c c c b a g a**

Try to find them on the lower frets of the guitar.

	= Strum down
	= Strum up

Accompaniment: 4/4 Rhythm

Chorus

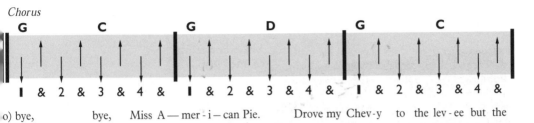

o) bye,   bye,   Miss A — mer - i — can Pie.   Drove my Chev-y   to the lev-ee but the

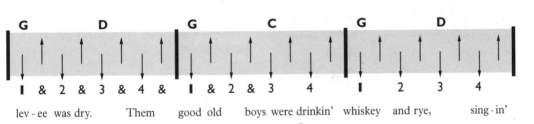

lev - ee was dry.   Them   good old   boys were drinkin'   whiskey   and rye,   sing - in'

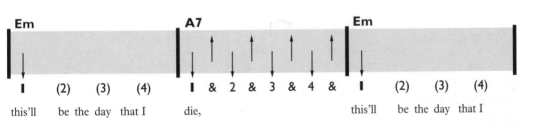

this'll   be the day that I   die,   this'll   be the day that I

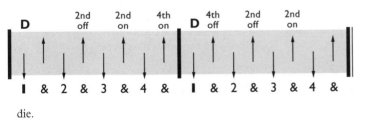

die.

Words & Music by Don McLean

53

Brown Eyed Girl

Van Morrison

Strumming Style

Half Bar Stress

Sometimes an offbeat stress is part of the main rhythmic feel of an accompaniment. Van Morrison's 'Brown Eyed Girl' requires a stress between the 2nd & 3rd beats. The stress in the middle of a bar is a very common place for syncopation and is found in many areas of modern music:

4/4 Rhythm Hold any chord

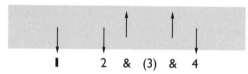

Make the upstrum between beats 2 & 3 a little longer than usual, i.e. four or five strings instead of two or three. To help you keep the rhythm you should do an 'airstroke' with your hand (or pick) on the 3rd beat. In other words move your hand downwards without touching the strings.

If you do strum on this beat it should be short and very light.

Speed

This accompaniment should be played quite fast, at about 155 beats per minute. The standard music expression for a fast tempo is 'allegro'.

Accompaniment: 4/4 Rhythm

The Bm Chord

The **Bm** chord is used in this arrangement. See page 3 for the fingering of this common barre chord.

Melody

String	⌐3rd⌐	4th	⌐3rd⌐	⌐———4th———⌐
Fret	2 0	4 0	2 4	2 0 2

Hey where did we go, days when the rains

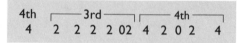

came, down in the hollow, playin' a new game.

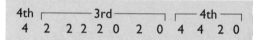

Laughin' and a-runnin', hey hey, skippin' and a-

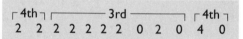

jumpin', in the misty mornin' fog with our, our

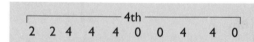

hearts a-thumpin', and you, my brown eyed girl.

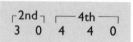

You, my brown eyed girl.

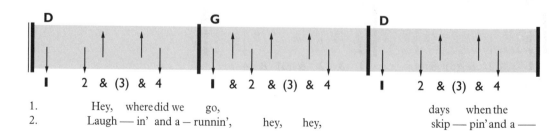

1.   Hey,   where did we   go,   days   when the
2.   Laugh — in' and a — runnin',   hey,   hey,   skip — pin' and a —

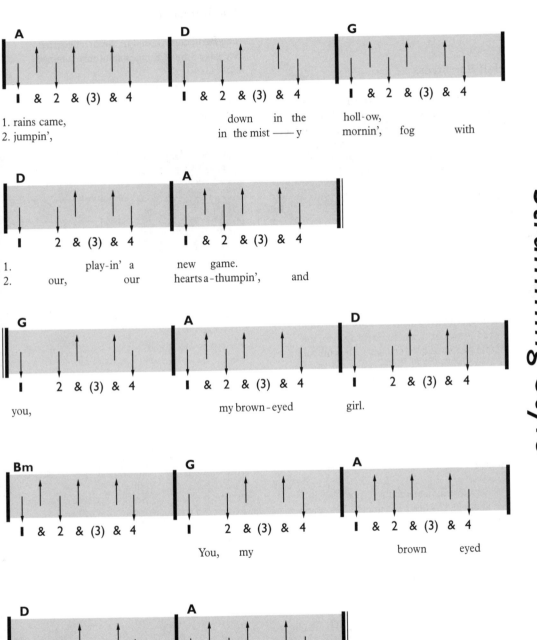

Strumming Style

Words & Music by Van Morrison

55

Eternal Flame

The Bangles

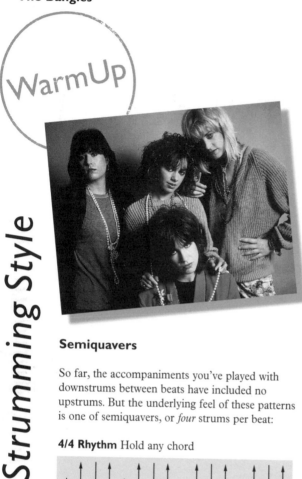

Strumming Style

Semiquavers

So far, the accompaniments you've played with downstrums between beats have included no upstrums. But the underlying feel of these patterns is one of semiquavers, or *four* strums per beat:

4/4 Rhythm Hold any chord

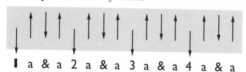

Play longer downstrums on each beat and stress each of them. Count the pattern as indicated. As with other strum patterns, you can remove some of the upstrums to produce a variety of rhythmic effects.

When you've mastered the combination I've given for the accompaniment, try some pattern variations of your own.

The F & Dm Chords

The **Bm** barre chord you played in the last accompaniment is also used in the verse of 'Eternal Flame'. You'll need to learn another common barre chord for the middle section of the song (shown at the end of Part 2). Together with **Bm**, the **F** chord is shown on page 49.

Another new chord you'll need to know for the middle section is **Dm**:

Dm Chord

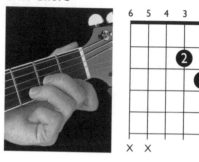

Melody

Check the melody of 'Eternal Flame' by picking out the notes shown below. Work out the note names and then try singing the melody. Male singers should find and sing the notes an octave lower.

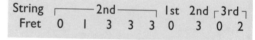

Close your eyes, give me your hand, darling

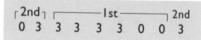

Do you feel my heart beating? Do you

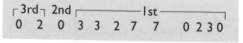

understand? Do you feel the same? Am I only

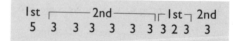

dreaming? Is this burning an eternal flame?

| | = Strum down |
| | = Strum up |

Accompaniment: 4/4 Rhythm

Verse

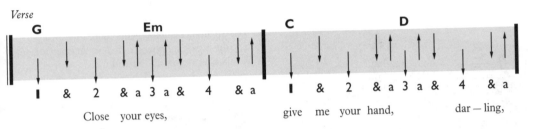

G   **Em**

1 & 2 & a 3 a & 4 & a

Close   your eyes,

C   **D**

1 & 2 & a 3 a & 4 & a

give   me   your hand,   dar — ling,

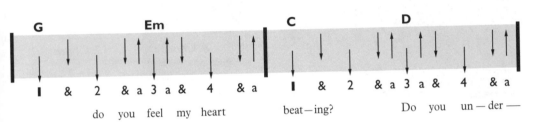

G   **Em**

1 & 2 & a 3 a & 4 & a

do   you   feel   my   heart

C   **D**

1 & 2 & a 3 a & 4 & a

beat — ing?   Do   you   un — der —

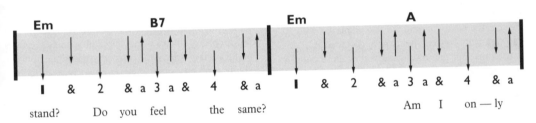

Em   **B7**

1 & 2 & a 3 a & 4 & a

stand?   Do   you   feel   the   same?

Em   **A**

1 & 2 & a 3 a & 4 & a

Am   I   on — ly

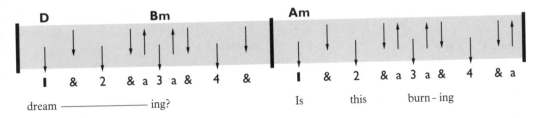

D   **Bm**

1 & 2 & a 3 a & 4 & &

dream ——————— ing?

Am

1 & 2 & a 3 a & 4 & a

Is   this   burn - ing

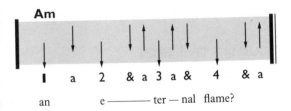

Am

1 a 2 & a 3 a & 4 & a

an   e ——— ter — nal flame?

Words & Music by Billy Steinberg, Tom Kelly & Susanna Hoffs
© Copyright 1988 & 1989 Billy Steinberg Music, Sony / ATV Tunes LLC & Bangophile Music, USA.
Sony / ATV Music Publishing (UK) Limited, 10 Great Marlborough Street, London W1 (66.66%) / Copyright Control (33.34%).
All Rights Reserved. International Copyright Secured.

More Ideas

Bass Runs

Bass runs are used to link chords and break up the usual bass-strum patterns. Try this run between the **A** and **D** chords:

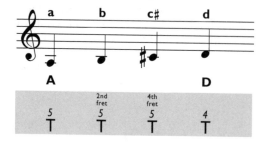

Use your 1st and 3rd fingers for the **b** & **c♯** notes. Moving back for a **D** to an **A** chord, the notes can be played in reverse. Similar runs can be used between other chords:

G to **C** = **g a b c** (on 6th & 5th strings)

D to **G** = **d e f♯ g** (for **e f♯** & **g** use 6th string)

E to **A** = **e f♯ g♯ a** (from 6th to 5th string)

C to **F** = **c d e f** (from 5th to 4th string)

Use your 2nd & 3rd fingers, except for **g♯** where the 4th finger is needed. Bass runs can also link a major and minor chord:

Am to **C** = **a b c** (5th string)

Em to **G** = **e f♯ g** (6th string)

Normally the first chord is held by the left hand until the fingers have to move to hold a fretted run note. When the final run note is played, the left hand is in the new chord position. Bass run notes have to be fitted into the 4/4 or 3/4 rhythm patterns in particular ways so they sound right. The next three songs show how this can be done.

When you've been through the accompaniments in this section, go back to the bass-strum section in Part 1 and spice up the accompaniments with some hammer-ons and bass runs.

The Hammer-on

The hammer-on is perhaps the most used of the guitar embellishments. After a first note has been sounded by the right hand striking a string, the left hand produces a second note by coming down firmly onto a higher fret. Lower string hammer-ons are easier to do and are often used to make bass-strum accompaniments more interesting. Try these examples which involve an open string with a hammer-on to the 2nd fret:

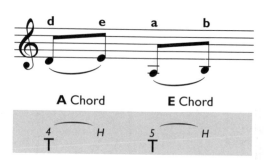

Use your 1st finger for the **E** note and 2nd finger for the **B**. Count the two notes '1 &'. Come down fast and firmly so the hammered note is clearly sounded. Now try fingering a whole **A** chord and do the same on the 4th string, then an **E** chord and do the same on the 5th string. Just raise the appropriate finger and hammer it down again.

Fretted notes of many chords will sound great when they are hammered down from an open string. Here are the chords you've learnt so far and the notes normally used for hammer-ons:

A Am A7 or **C: d** to **e** (4th string)

A Am D or **Dm: g** to **a** (3rd string)

G E Em E7 or **B7: a** to **b** (5th string)

You'll notice that these common hammer-on notes are a tone apart in pitch (two frets on the guitar).

Using A Thumbpick

If you want to make the bass notes stand out, but don't feel comfortable with a flatpick for the bass-strum style, you could try using a thumbpick. It's always worth experimenting with different approaches which can produce varied effects.

Country Waltz

Russ Shipton

$\overset{4\frown H}{T}$ =	Thumb plays 4th string left hand hammers-on
↓	= Strum down
↑	= Strum up

Bass Runs And Hammer-ons
In 3/4 Rhythm

This instrumental illustrates how bass runs and hammer-ons can be used in the 3/4 rhythm. Follow the fret and string numbers above the thumb indications carefully.

For the **A** to **E** bass run in bar 6 and the **A** to **D** run in bar 10, take your hand off the chord after the 1st beat and be in the new chord position for the 1st beat of the next bar. The **E** to **A** run in bar 14 involves moving the left hand after the strum on beat 2. Then use your 1st finger for the 2nd fret **f♯** note and hammer your 3rd finger down for the **g♯** on the 4th fret.

All the other hammer-ons are from an open string to the usual fretted note for the chord.

Accompaniment: 3/4 Rhythm

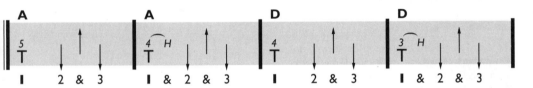

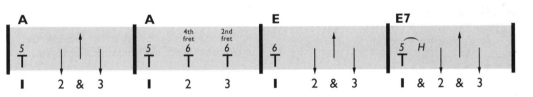

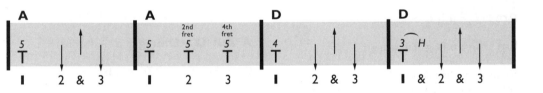

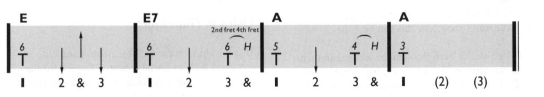

Bass-Strum Style

Dedicated Follower Of Fashion

The Kinks

More Chords

You now need to learn four new chords for this next accompaniment.

Csus4 Chord

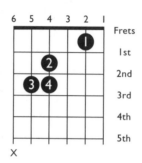

G7 Chord

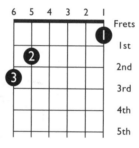

A7 Chord

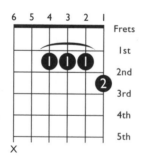

Dm7 Chord

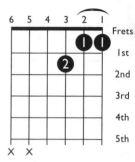

The **Csus4** means adding an **f** note temporarily to the usual **C** chord (with the 4th finger). The **G7** is straightforward. The **A7** is another version, this time involving a short bar. The **Dm7** (**D** minor seventh) involves adding another note to the standard minor chord. Here this means using a short bar.

Bass Runs In 4/4 Rhythm

This arrangement provides some ideas on how to fit bass runs into 4/4 bass-strum patterns. Follow the bass string and fret indications carefully and take your hand off the chord only when you need to. Be in the new chord for the last note of each run.

Lead-In

The Kinks use a strumming style lead-in, with strums on just beats 1 & 3. Tap your foot on each beat and count the rhythm carefully. After verse 1 return to bar 3 of the lead-in to begin verse 2. The chorus is given on page 82.

Accompaniment: 4/4 Rhythm

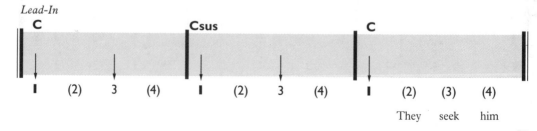

Verse

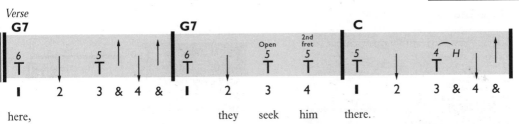

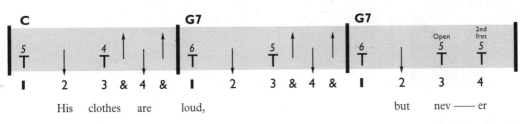

Bass-Strum Style

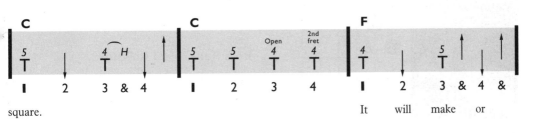

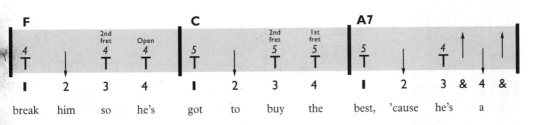

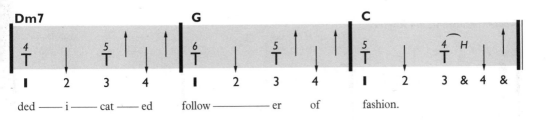

Words & Music by Ray Davies

Like A Rolling Stone

Bob Dylan

Bass-Strum Style (vertical text, left margin)

'Slow' Bass Runs

This arrangement involves rising and falling bass runs, but here the notes of the runs come on every other beat. Follow the bass string and fret indications and the **c d e** & **f** run from the 5th to 4th strings will emerge.

Pattern Changes And Repeats

Semiquaver strums are included in this accompaniment. Watch out for all the typical Dylan repetition of lines which helps to get his message over more forcefully. The last two bars shown for the chorus need to be played 5 times, the last time instrumentally after you've sung 'stone'.

Try using a flatpick instead of thumb and fingers if you want to produce a heavier sound.

Accompaniment: 4/4 Rhythm

Verse

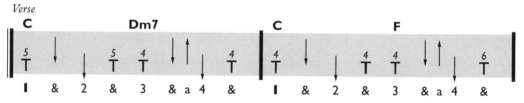

1. Once upon   a time you dressed so   fine   you   threw the bums a dime,   in your prime,
2.   people'd call,   say 'Be — ware, doll, you're bound to fall',   you thought they were all

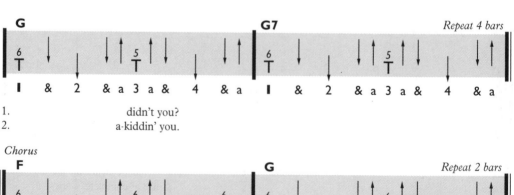

1.   didn't you?
2.   a-kiddin' you.

Chorus

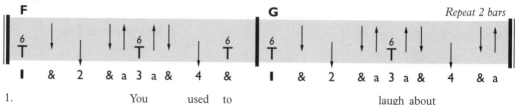

1.   You   used   to   laugh about
2.   ev'ry-body that   was   hangin' out.

$\overset{5}{T}$ = Thumb plays 5th string
↓ = Strum down
↑ = Strum up

Bass-Strum Style

F   **C**   **Dm7**   **C**   *Repeat 2 bars*

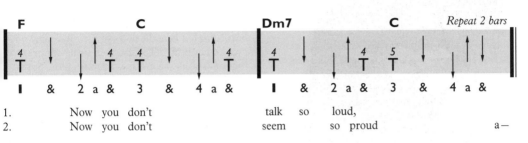

1 & 2 a & 3 & 4 a &   1 & 2 a & 3 & 4 a &

1.   Now you don't   talk so loud,
2.   Now you don't   seem so proud   a—

F   **F**

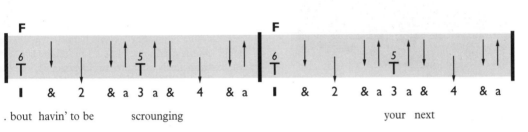

1 & 2 & a 3 a & 4 & a   1 & 2 & a 3 a & 4 & a

. bout havin' to be   scrounging   your next

G   **G**

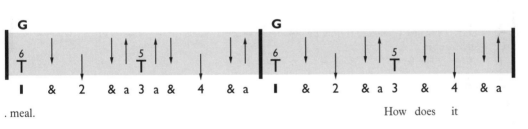

1 & 2 & a 3 a & 4 & a   1 & 2 & a 3 & 4 & a

. meal.   How does it

Chorus

C   **F**   **G**   *Repeat 2 bars x 4*

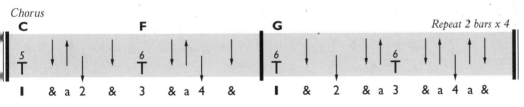

1 & a 2 & 3 & a 4 &   1 & 2 & a 3 & a 4 a &

1. feel,   how does it
2. feel,   to be without a
3. home   like a complete un —
4. known,   like a rolling   stone.

More Ideas

Arpeggio Style

Bass Runs

Like the bass-strum style, bass runs can be included in arpeggio patterns to make things more interesting. They can be two, three or four notes in length. Two-note runs are used in the accompaniment opposite for 'The House Of The Risin' Sun'. You could try using a three-note run linking the **Am** & **C** chords:

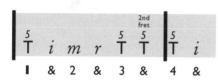

Here is an example of a four-note run in the 3/4 rhythm, from **A** to **D**:

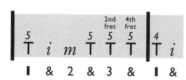

'Slow' runs can also be used in the arpeggio style, as you'll see in the arrangement for 'Sailing'. The run notes can fall on every beat (or even every other beat) instead of on and off the beat.

The 6/8 Rhythm

A number of rock, pop and blues songs are arranged with a 6/8 rhythm. The '6' means there are six beats per bar and the '8' means that each beat lasts for a quaver. This kind of rhythm is called a 'compound' rhythm because each bar is divided into two groups of three. You stress the 1st and 4th beats:

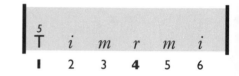

Notice the difference in stress points between the 3/4 rhythm and the 6/8 rhythm. The Animals played their version of 'The House Of The Risin' Sun' with the 6/8 rhythm, but they added a semiquaver note:

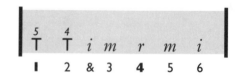

The Hammer-on

The hammer-on in the arpeggio style is usually played as a semiquaver, squeezed into a halfbeat:

The House Of The Rising Sun

Traditional, arranged by Russ Shipton

T	= Thumb
i	= Index finger
m	= Middle finger
r	= Ring finger

Accompaniment: 3/4 Rhythm

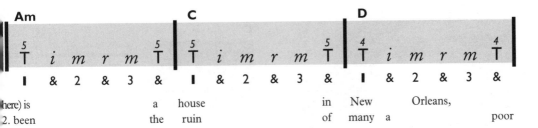

Am
5 T *i* *m* *r* *m* 5 T
| & 2 & 3 &

here) is .... a house .... in New .... Orleans,
2. been .... the ruin .... of many a .... poor

C
5 T *i* *m* *r* *m* 5 T

D
4 T *i* *m* *r* *m* 4 T

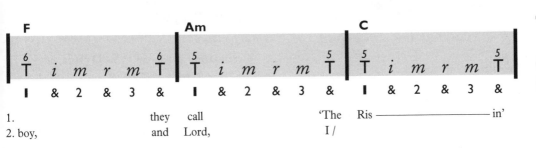

F
6 T *i* *m* *r* *m* 6 T
| & 2 & 3 &

1. .... they call
2. boy, ... and Lord,

Am
5 T *i* *m* *r* *m* 5 T
| & 2 & 3 &

'The Ris ——————— in'
I /

C
5 T *i* *m* *r* *m* 5 T
| & 2 & 3 &

E
6 T *i* *m* *r* *m* *i*
| & 2 & 3 &

Sun',

E7 *Repeat first 5 bars*
5 H
T *i* *m* *r* *m* *i*
| a & 2 & 3 &

and it's

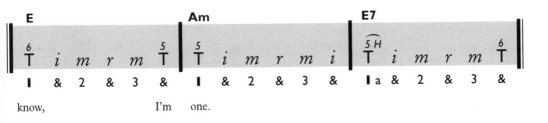

E
6 T *i* *m* *r* *m* 5 T
| & 2 & 3 &

know, ... I'm one.

Am
5 T *i* *m* *r* *m* *i*
| & 2 & 3 &

E7
5 H
T *i* *m* *r* *m* 6 T
| a & 2 & 3 &

Arpeggio Style

Sailing

Rod Stewart

Arpeggio Style

A New Chord

The **D** chord is sometimes replaced by the **D7** when in the key of **G** major:

D7 Chord

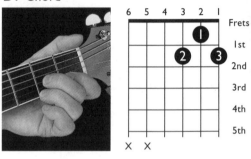

The fingering is different to the **D** chord, but just one note has changed.

In the 2nd bar of the lead-in you need to remove your 2nd finger from the top string, then put it back. This produces a treble run. The right hand thumb and all three fingers are used for the **D** chord at the end of the lead-in and for the **D7** at the end of the verse.

Standard Notation

This great ballad made famous by Rod Stewart involves an interesting but straightforward chord sequence in the arpeggio style. I've shown it in standard notation so you can get some practice reading the notes and finding them on the guitar.

One of the patterns you know forms the basis of the accompaniment, and there are hammer-ons (shown by small curved lines) and bass runs included to make the arrangement more interesting. All the 6th, 5th & 4th string notes are played by the right hand thumb as usual.

Melody

When you can play the accompaniment for 'Sailing', try singing as well. To help you get started, the notes for the first line are shown below. Try to find them on the lower frets.

g g b d e e

Accompaniment: 4/4 Rhythm

Words & Music by Gavin Sutherland
© Copyright 1972 Island Music Limited Universal/Island Music Limited, 77 Fulham Palace Road, London W6.
All Rights Reserved. International Copyright Secured.

Can't Help Falling In Love

Elvis Presley

Arpeggio Style

6/8 Picking Patterns

Both Elvis Presley and UB40 have recorded popular versions of this song. The original was written in the 6/8 rhythm, as shown here. Stress the 1st & 4th beats and you'll produce the correct rhythmic feel for the song. Bass runs and hammer-ons are included in much the same way as in the 3/4 arpeggio patterns. Follow the string and fret indications carefully.

6/8 Strumming Patterns

Sometimes guitarists will vary an accompaniment by using a picking style for the verse and strumming for the chorus or middle section.

For the middle section of this song you could use this simple 6/8 strumming pattern:

6/8 Rhythm Finger an **Em** Chord

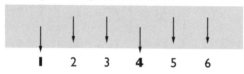

Make the strums on beats 1 & 4 longer and heavier.

The pattern I've given for the middle section opposite includes an upstrum between beats 5 & 6. The strum on beat 5 and the upstrum following are both semiquavers and should be played quickly. Follow the count given. When you can play the arrangement as given, you could try varying the main pattern by switching the order of the right hand fingers. You could also try adding your own hammer-ons and runs.

Other 6/8 Songs

Though the 6/8 rhythm is not as common as 4/4 and 3/4, there have been quite a few successful songs written in this rhythm. Pop hits include REM's 'Everybody Hurts', Elton John's 'I Guess That's Why They Call It The Blues', The Moody Blues' 'Nights In White Satin', 'Memory' from 'Cats', Jonathan King's 'Everyone's Gone To The Moon' and the Beatles' 'Baby's In Black'. There are many blues songs in 6/8, including Gary Moore's 'I've Still Got The Blues For You', and a number of traditional songs like 'The Mountains Of Mourne' and 'The Black Velvet Band'. Try picking or strumming a few of these songs when you can play this accompaniment.

Melody

Here are the notes for the first line. Try to find them on the lower frets:

c g c d e f e d

Accompaniment: 6/8 Rhythm

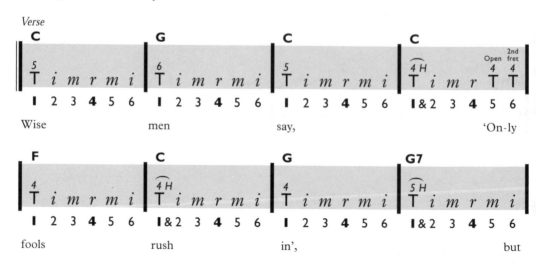

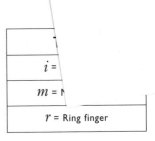

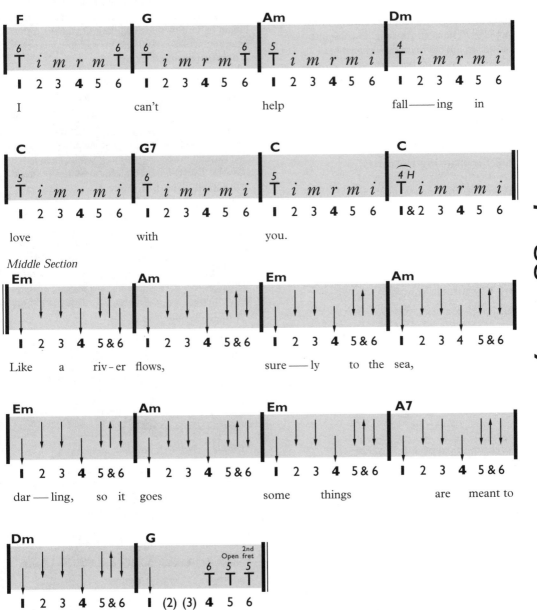

Arpeggio Style

| F | G | Am | Dm |

⁶T i m r m ⁶T ⁶T i m r m ⁶T ⁵T i m r m i ⁴T i m r m i

1 2 3 **4** 5 6   **1** 2 3 **4** 5 6   **1** 2 3 **4** 5 6   **1** 2 3 **4** 5 6

I   can't   help   fall——ing   in

| C | G7 | C | C |

⁵T i m r m i ⁶T i m r m i ⁵T i m r m i ⁴H T i m r m i

1 2 3 **4** 5 6   **1** 2 3 **4** 5 6   **1** 2 3 **4** 5 6   **1**&2 3 **4** 5 6

love   with   you.

Middle Section

| Em | Am | Em | Am |

1 2 3 **4** 5 & 6   **1** 2 3 **4** 5 & 6   **1** 2 3 **4** 5 & 6   **1** 2 3 **4** 5 & 6

Like   a   riv-er   flows,   sure——ly   to   the   sea,

| Em | Am | Em | A7 |

1 2 3 **4** 5 & 6   **1** 2 3 **4** 5 & 6   **1** 2 3 **4** 5 & 6   **1** 2 3 **4** 5 & 6

dar——ling,   so   it   goes   some   things   are   meant to

| Dm | G |

                                      Open 2nd fret

                             ⁶T ⁵T ⁵T

1 2 3 **4** 5 & 6   **1** (2) (3) **4** 5 6

be.

Words & Music by George Weiss, Hugo Peretti & Luigi Creatore

© Copyright 1961 Gladys Music, USA.

Manor Music Company Limited, Iron Bridge House, 3 Bridge Approach, London NW1 for the United Kingdom,

Eire, Israel & the British Dominions, Colonies, Overseas Territories & Dependencies (excluding Canada, Australia and New Zealand).

All Rights Reserved. International Copyright Secured.

How To Do It

The main exponents of the alternating thumb style are folk and country pickers, like Bob Dylan, Ralph McTell and Paul Simon. There are also many blues and ragtime players who use this style, including Stefan Grossman, John Fahey, Reverend Gary Davis, Blind Blake and Mississippi John Hurt.

The essential ingredient of this style is the alternating bass part. Normally a lower bass note is followed by a higher one and the two are repeated. Hold an **E** chord and play this sequence over and over again, keeping the beats even and the speed moderate:

4/4 Rhythm Finger an **E** Chord

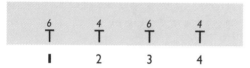

Don't move your right hand too much or you'll find it more difficult to strike the right string every time. While the bass notes give you a rocking and steady underlying rhythmic feel, treble notes can be added to harmonise with what you're singing. (When you become accomplished at this style, it is also possible to pick out part or the whole of a song melody, as you'll see later in the course). Try this simple pattern with just two treble notes added to the bass part:

4/4 Rhythm Finger an **E** Chord

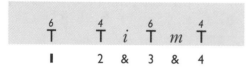

For the moment use just two right hand fingers. *The index finger will always strike the 2nd string and the middle finger the 1st string.* Count the pattern carefully and play it quite slowly to begin with. As usual you must make sure that the beats are evenly spaced. When you have this alternating thumb pattern under control, enjoy playing 'Jolene' and 'Streets Of London'.

Simple 4/4 Pattern Sequence
Finger an **E** Chord

Thumb strikes 6th string

Thumb strikes 4th string

1st finger strikes 2nd string

Thumb strikes 6th string

2nd finger strikes 1st string

Thumb strikes 4th string

Jolene

Dolly Parton

Bass And Treble Variations

When you can play this accompaniment, try different bass strings for the 2nd, 3rd, and 4th beats. (Normally the 'root' note comes on the 1st beat, i.e. the note with the same name as the chord.) Also try creating new patterns by adding or removing treble notes.

Melody

The notes for the first line of the chorus are:

g a b c c d g a g e

Accompaniment: 4/4 Rhythm

Alternating Thumb Style

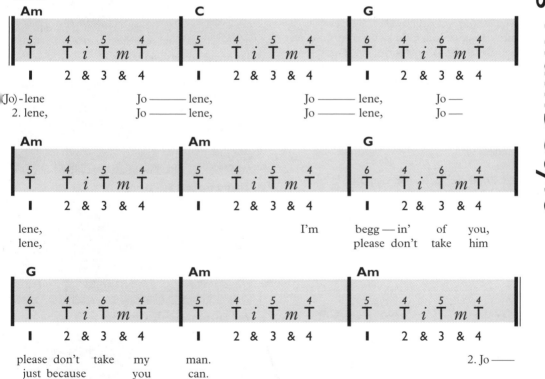

Words & Music by Dolly Parton

Streets Of London

Ralph McTell

Alternating Thumb Style

The Pinch

Ralph McTell uses the alternating thumb style for many songs. This arrangement is simpler than his, but he uses a 'pinch' at the start of his main pattern, so I've included this in each bar.

The pinch is indicated by a large 'P'. The number above it is the string to be struck by the thumb. The 1st string is played by the middle finger at the same time. The action of thumb and finger gives the pinch its name.

Different Patterns

Notice that the verse involves just one pattern and the chorus has alternating patterns. Follow the count beneath the notation carefully.

The Complete Guitar Player Tablature Book

There are many intermediate and advanced arrangements in The Complete Guitar Player Tablature Book, including Ralph McTell's original recorded version of 'Streets Of London'.

Accompaniment: 4/4 Rhythm

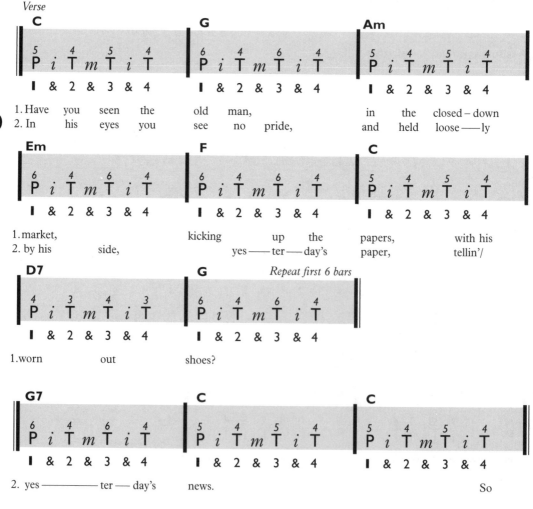

Verse

C
5 P 4 i T 5 m T 4 i T
1 & 2 & 3 & 4
1. Have you seen the
2. In his eyes you

G
6 P 4 i T 6 m T 4 i T
1 & 2 & 3 & 4
old man,
see no pride,

Am
5 P 4 i T 5 m T 4 i T
1 & 2 & 3 & 4
in the closed – down
and held loose —— ly

Em
6 P 4 i T 6 m T 4 i T
1 & 2 & 3 & 4
1. market,
2. by his side,

F
6 P 4 i T 6 m T 4 i T
1 & 2 & 3 & 4
kicking up the
yes —— ter —— day's

C
5 P 4 i T 5 m T 4 i T
1 & 2 & 3 & 4
papers, with his
paper, tellin'/

D7
4 P 3 i T 4 m T 3 i T
1 & 2 & 3 & 4
1. worn out

G *Repeat first 6 bars*
6 P 4 i T 6 m T 4 i T
1 & 2 & 3 & 4
shoes?

G7
6 P 4 i T 6 m T 4 i T
1 & 2 & 3 & 4
2. yes ———— ter — day's

C
5 P 4 i T 5 m T 4 i T
1 & 2 & 3 & 4
news.

C
5 P 4 i T 5 m T 4 i T
1 & 2 & 3 & 4
So

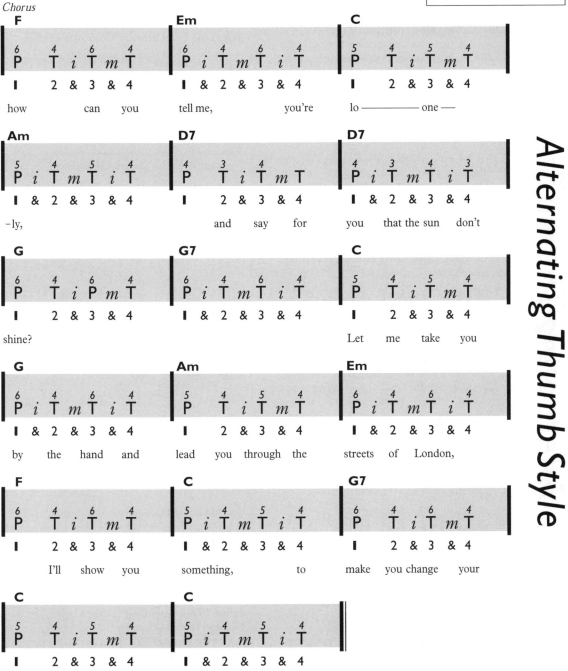

Alternating Thumb Style

Summary

Alternating Thumb Style

Alternating Bass Notes

As mentioned on page 71, the **root** note of a chord is normally the bass note that begins an alternating thumb pattern. This is the low note that has the same name as the chord. Here are the bass strings that are most commonly played with particular chords:

E Em E7 F G and **G7** all have their root note on the 6th string. *The 6th & 4th strings are normally played for these chords*, but the 6th & 3rd might also be used. Other possibilities are: 6th 4th 5th 4th, 6th 3rd 5th 3rd, 6th 3rd 4th 3rd, or 6th 3rd 6th 4th.

A Am A7 B7 Bm and **C** all have their root note on the 5th string. *The 5th & 4th strings are normally played for these chords*, but the 5th & 3rd might also be used. Other possibilities are: 5th 4th 5th 3rd, 5th 3rd 5th 4th, 5th 4th 6th 4th or 5th 3rd 6th 3rd. The last two are only possible with the **C** chord if the 3rd finger moves to the 3rd fret of the 6th string.

D Dm Dm7 and **D7** all have their root note on the 4th string. *The 4th & 3rd strings are normally played for these chords.* Another possibility is 4th 3rd 5th 3rd.

Try changing the bass strings but for the moment use just the top two strings for the treble notes. Patterns with all three treble strings will be looked at in Part 3.

Different Patterns

Here are a number of patterns for you to play over and over until you can play them quickly and smoothly. Try using different keys and play the patterns with all the chords you know. Try working out some patterns for yourself.

4/4 Rhythm Hold any chord

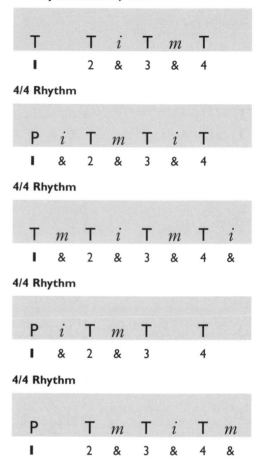

Other Alternating Thumb Songs

Here are some other songs that you might like to try playing with simple alternating patterns:

One Too Many Mornings (Bob Dylan)
Don't Think Twice It's All Right (Bob Dylan)
Girl Of The North Country (Bob Dylan)
Homeward Bound (Paul Simon)
April Come She Will (Paul Simon)
The Boxer (Paul Simon)
Leaves That Are Green (Paul Simon)
Ballad Of A Crystal Man (Donovan)
Four And Twenty (Stephen Stills)
Last Thing On My Mind (Tom Paxton)
Speed Of The Sound Of Loneliness (John Prine)
Castles In The Air (Don McLean)
From Clare To Here (Ralph McTell)
Life Time Lover (Jim Croce)

How To Do It

In fact, there are many different 'ways' of playing the guitar in a classical style, as there are in the other main areas of guitar music. But there's no obvious divisions like strumming, bass-strum, arpeggio and alternating thumb.

Maybe then you could say that the difference between the classical and other styles of playing is that it is more random - it doesn't stick to patterns anywhere near as much as folk or modern guitar music. There is of course another very important difference - almost always classical music is 'instrumental' only. It isn't an accompaniment for a song.

When a piece is an instrumental, it's *extremely* important to get the notes clear and to give them their full time value. It is of course very important to play all types of music well, but perhaps this classical study on the next page (and others in Part 3) will help you to concentrate on making the most of what you're playing.

Have a look at the first bar - can you remember how long the notes should last? If you've been working out or checking parts of the song melodies so far, you should know the pitch of the notes on the treble clef too...

*This means there are **4 beats** in each bar (i.e. 4 foot taps)*

This means that the length of each beat is one crotchet (4 crotchets in each bar)

Fingers

There are no hard and fast rules on which right hand finger you should use, but when two notes are played after each other on the same string, it's often a good idea for smoothness to swap fingers. I'll indicate which finger I think you should use, above each note.

As for the left hand, classical players put down only the fingers they need at the time. Other players normally use the usual whole chord shape. In fact with classical music, the emphasis is not on chords at all.

The finger that you must use for each note in this piece will be the *same as the fret number* i.e. if the note is on the 1st fret, then you must use your 1st finger, if the note's on the 2nd fret, you use your 2nd finger and so on. Only the first three frets are used in this one, so you'll only have to use your first three left hand fingers.

Finding The Notes On The Guitar

As you've been doing when finding and playing the melody notes of the songs, look for the lowest position for each note. In fact, in this piece, the 3rd fret is the highest that you go, so they'll be quite easy to find!

In the classical style the thumb must be kept clear of the fingers.

Study

Fernando Sor

Reading The Notes

Your first classical piece, a study by a famous composer and guitarist of the early 19th century, is shown in standard notation. Take each separately to start with and make sure you find the right fret for each note.

All the notes should be played at the lowest fret possible. Many notes can be played with an open string. The timing is quite easy: four beats to a bar and just minims (two beats) and crotchets (one beat) throughout.

Fingering

The fingering for the right hand is shown above the notation. The left hand fingering is straightforward. Use the 1st finger for the 1st fret notes, the 2nd finger for the 2nd fret notes and the 3rd finger for the 3rd fret notes.

Note Length

Try to make each note last as long as the music says it should last. In other words, don't take your finger off as soon as you've played the note. It's often better to leave one finger where it is until the next has been played. The sound can then be much smoother.

T = Thumb	
i = Index finger	
m = Middle finger	
r = Ring finger	

Instrumental: 4/4 Rhythm

Section One

This sign means 'repeat'. In this case you go back to the start and play all 8 bars of section 1 again.

Section Two

Repeat Section Two

By Fernando Sor

The Major Scale

c note (low) / d note (open 4th string)

Before going on to Part 3, I'd like you to think about the Do Re Mi etc. that you've all sung at one time or another. It's the major scale that you're singing, but which one depends on which note is the starting note. All major scales sound similar in an overall way because the spaces or intervals between the notes are always the same. Let's have a look at the **C** major scale - that's the one where we don't have to bother with flats or sharps...

The C Major Scale

    c   d   e   f   g   a   b   c

e note

To play this scale on your guitar, start by putting your 3rd finger on the left hand on the 3rd fret of the 5th string. Alternate the first two right hand fingers (don't bother with the thumb for this exercise), and use the usual left hand fingers on the appropriate frets.

When you've worked out where the notes are for the left hand, and you've played the **C** scale smoothly through a couple of times, can you work out which notes from this scale are used for the **C** chord (or **C** major chord, to give its full name)? Also, what *are* the intervals between the notes of a major scale (that are always the same)? And what's the total interval in both frets and tones between the low **c** and high **c** notes?

f note / g note (open 3rd string)

Now see if you can write out the **G** major scale in the same way as I've written the **C** scale above. If you keep the intervals between the notes in the same order, you should find one note that has to be 'sharpened' i.e. raised in pitch by a semitone, or fret. And then can you play it on the guitar?

These scales are extremely important because the chords and melody notes you've been playing come from scales. Try to remember the intervals of the major scale before moving on to Part 3.

a note / b note (open 2nd string)

c note (high)

Useful Information

Yellow Submarine

Verse 1
In the town where I was born
Lived a man who sailed to sea
And he told us of his life
In the land of submarines.

Verse 2
So we sailed up to the sun
Till we found a sea of green
And we lived beneath the waves
In our yellow submarine.

Chorus
We all live in a yellow submarine
Yellow submarine
Yellow submarine.
We all live in a yellow submarine
Yellow submarine
Yellow submarine.

Verse 3
And our friends are all aboard
Many more of them live next door
And the band begins to play...

Verse 4
As we live a life of ease
Every one of us has all we need
Sky of blue, sea of green
In our yellow submarine.

Lyrics

American Pie

Verse 1 (ad lib rhythm)

 G   D   Em   Am   C
A long, long time ago, I can still remember
                Em   D
how that music used to make me smile
 G   D   Em
And I knew if I had my chance
     Am   C
that I could make those people dance
         Em   C   D
and maybe they'd be happy for a while

Em   Am
But February made me shiver
Em   Am
with every paper I'd deliver
C   G   Am
Bad news on the doorstep
          C   D
I couldn't take one more step
G   D   Em
I can't remember if I cried
       Am   D
when I read about his widowed bride
G   D   Em
But something touched me deep inside
          C   D   G
the day the music died.

Chorus
So bye, bye, Miss American Pie
Drove my Chevy to the levee but the levee was dry
Them good old boys were drinkin' whiskey and rye
Singin' this'll be the day that I die
This'll be the day that I die.

Verse 2
 G   Am
Did you write the book of love
          C   Am
and do you have faith in God above
Em   D
if the bible tells you so?
        G   D   Em
Now do you believe in rock and roll,
         Am   C
can music save your mortal soul?
         Em   A7   D
And can you teach me how to dance real slow?
         Em   D
Well I know that you're in love with him,
              Em   D
'cause I saw you dancin' in the gym
         C   G   A7
You both kicked off your shoes,
              C   D
man I dig those rhythm and blues
         G   D   Em
I was a lonely, teenage broncin' buck
              Am   C
with a pink carnation and a pickup truck
         G   D   Em   C   D G C G
But I knew I was out of luck the day the music died,
              D
I started singin'...

Verse 3
Now for ten years we've been on our own
      and moss grows fat on a rollin' stone
But that's not how it used to be
      when the jester sang for the king and queen
In a coat he borrowed from James Dean
      and a voice that came from you and me
Oh and while the king was looking down
      the jester stole his thorny crown
The courtroom was adjourned
      no verdict was returned
And while Lennon read a book on Marx
      the quartet practised in the park
And we sang dirges in the dark
We were singin'...

Verse 4

Helter-skelter in the summer swelter
    the Byrds flew off with a fallout shelter
Eight miles high and fallin' fast
    it landed foul on the grass
The players tried for a forward pass
    with a jester on the sidelines in a cast
Now the halftime air was sweet perfume while the
    sergeants played a marching tune
We all got up to dance
    but we never got the chance
'Cause the players tried to take the field
    the marching band refused to yield
Do you recall what was revealed
    the day the music died?
We started singin'...

Verse 5

And there we were all in one place
    a generation lost in space
With no time left to start again
So come on, Jack be nimble, Jack be quick
    Jack Flash sat on a candlestick
'Cause fire is the devil's only friend
And as I watched him on the stage
    my hands were clenched in fists of rage
No angel born in hell
    could break that Satan's spell
And as the flames climbed high into the night
    to light the sacrificial rite
I saw Satan laughing with delight
    the day the music died
He was singin'...

Verse 6 (ad lib rhythm, as Verse 1)

I met a girl who sang the blues
    and I asked her for some happy news
But she just smiled and turned away
I went down to the sacred store
    where I heard the music years before
But the man there said the music wouldn't play
And in the streets the children screamed
    the lovers cried and the poets dreamed
But not a word was spoken
    the church bells all were broken
And the three men I admire most
    the Father, Son and the Holy Ghost
They caught the last train for the coast
    the day the music died
And they were singin'...

Brown Eyed Girl

Verse 1

Hey where did we go, days when the rains came
Down in the hollow, playin' a new game
Laughing and a-running, hey hey
    skipping and a-jumping
In the misty morning fog with our
Our hearts a-thumping and you
My brown eyed girl
You, my brown eyed girl.

Verse 2

Whatever happened to Tuesday and so slow
Going down the old mine with a transistor radio
Standing in the sunlight, laughing
    hiding behind a rainbow's wall
Slipping and a-sliding all along
    the waterfall with you
My brown eyed girl
You, my brown eyed girl.

Middle Section

D   **D**   **D**   **G**
Do you remember when we used to sing
      C   **G**   **D**   **G**
'Sha la la, la la la la, la la la la te da
      C   **G**   **D**   **G**
Sha la la, la la la la, la la la la te da, la te da.

Verse 3

So hard to find my way, now that I'm all on my own
I saw you just the other day, my, how you have grown
Cast my memory back there, Lord, sometimes
    I'm overcome just thinking 'bout it
Makin' love in the green grass
    behind the stadium with you
My brown eyed girl
You, my brown eyed girl.

Eternal Flame

Verse 1
Close your eyes, give me your hand, darling
Do you feel my heart beating?
Do you understand?
Do you feel the same, am I only dreaming
Is this burning an eternal flame?

Verse 2
I believe it's meant to be, darling
I watch you when you are sleeping
You belong with me
Do you feel the same?
Am I only dreaming
Or is this burning an eternal flame?

Middle section
D   Dm G   D
Say my name, sun shines through the rain
       F   G
A whole life so lonely and then
  C   Am
Come and ease the pain
D   Bm   F C D
I don't wanna lose this feeling, oh.

Em B7 Em A7

Dedicated Follower Of Fashion

Verse 1
They seek him here, they seek him there
His clothes are loud, but never square
It will make or break him so he's got to buy the best
'Cause he's a dedicated follower of fashion.

Verse 2
And when he does his little rounds
Round the boutiques of London Town
Eagerly pursuing all the latest fads and trends
'Cause he's a dedicated follower of fashion.

Chorus
C   G G7   C
Oh yes he is, oh yes he is
            F   F   C
He thinks he is a flower to be looked at
            F   F
And when he pulls his frilly nylon
        C   (run)   A7
panties right up tight,
                Dm7   G7   C
He feels a dedicated follower of fashion.

Chorus (2)
Oh yes he is, oh yes he is
There's one thing that he loves and that is flattery
One week he's in polka dots
        the next week he's in stripes
'Cause he's a dedicated follower of fashion.

Verse 3
They seek him here, they seek him there
In Regent Street and Leicester Square
Everywhere the Carnabytion Army marches on
Each one a dedicated follower of fashion.

Chorus (3)
Oh yes he is, oh yes he is
His world is built round discotheques and parties
This pleasure seeking individual always looks his best
'Cause he's a dedicated follower of fashion.

Chorus (4)
Oh yes he is, oh yes he is
He flits from shop to shop just like a butterfly
In matters of the cloth he is as fickle as can be
'Cause he's a dedicated follower of fashion.

Like A Rolling Stone

Verse 1

Once upon a time you dressed so fine
You threw the bums a dime, in your prime
Didn't you?
People'd call, say 'Beware doll, you're bound to fall'
You thought they were all kiddin' you
You used to laugh about everybody that was
    hangin' out
Now you don't talk so loud
Now you don't seem so proud
About having to be scrounging
For your next meal.

Chorus

How does it feel
How does it feel
To be without a home
Like a complete unknown
Like a rolling stone?

Verse 2

You've gone to the finest school all right
Miss Lonely, but you know you only used to get
Juiced in it
And nobody's ever taught you how to live out on
    the street
And now you're gonna have to get used to it
You said you'd never compromise
With the mystery tramp, but now you realise
He's not selling any alibis
As you stare into the vacuum of his eyes
And say
'Do you want to make a deal?'

Chorus 2

How does it feel
How does it feel
To be on your own
With no direction home
Like a complete unknown
Like a rolling stone?

Verse 3

You never turned around to see the frowns
    on the jugglers and the clowns
When they all did tricks for you
You never understood that it ain't no good
You shouldn't let other people get your kicks for you
You used to ride on the chrome horse with your
    diplomat
Who carried on his shoulder a Siamese cat
Ain't it hard when you discovered that
He really wasn't where it's at
After he took from you everything he could steal?

Verse 4

Princess on the steeple and all the pretty
    people they are drinkin'
Thinkin', that they got it made
Exchanging all precious gifts and things
But you'd better take your diamond ring
You'd better pawn it babe
You used to be so amused at Napoleon in rags
And the language that he used
Go to him now, he calls you, you can't refuse
When you got nothing, you got nothing to lose
You're invisible now
You got no secrets to conceal.

The House Of The Rising Sun

Verse 1

There is a house in New Orleans
They call 'The Risin' Sun'
And it's been the ruin of many a poor boy
And God, I know, I'm one.

Verse 2

My mother was a tailor
Sewed my new blue jeans
My father was a gamblin' man
Down in New Orleans.

Verse 3

Now the only thing to gamblin'
Is a suitcase and a trunk
And the only time he's satisfied
Is when he's on a drunk.

Verse 4

Go tell my baby sister
Not to do what I have done
To shun that house in New Orleans
They call 'The Risin' Sun'.

Verse 5

One foot on the platform
The other's on the train
I'm goin' back to New Orleans
To wear that ball and chain.

Lyrics

83

Lyrics

Sailing

Verse 1
I am sailing, I am sailing
Home again 'cross the sea
I am sailing stormy waters
To be near you, to be free.

Verse 2
I am flying, I am flying
Like a bird 'cross the sky
I am flying, passing high clouds
To be near you, to be free.

Verse 3
Can you hear me, can you hear me
Through the dark night, far away?
I am dying, forever crying
To be with you, who can say?

Verse 4
Can you hear me, can you hear me
Through the dark night, far away?
I am dying, forever crying
To be with you, who can say?

Verse 5
We are sailing, we are sailing
Home again 'cross the sea
We are sailing stormy waters
To be near you, to be free.

Can't Help Falling In Love

Verse 1
Wise men say
'Only fools rush in'
But I can't help
Falling in love with you.

Verse 2
Shall I stay
Would it be a sin
If I can't help
Falling in love with you?

Middle Section
Like a river flows
Surely to the sea
Darling, so it goes
Some things are meant to be.

Verse 3
Take my hand
Take my whole life too
For I can't help
Falling in love with you.

Jolene

Chorus
Jolene, Jolene, Jolene, Jolene
I'm beggin' of you, please don't take my man
Jolene, Jolene, Jolene, Jolene
Please don't take him just because you can.

Verse 1
    Am   **C**
Your beauty is beyond compare
       G   **Am**
With flaming locks of auburn hair
    G   **G**   **Am Am**
With ivory skin and eyes of emerald green
    Am   **C**
Your smile is like a breath of spring
     G   **Am**
Your voice is soft like summer rain
    G   **G**   **Am Am**
And I cannot compete with you, Jolene.

Verse 2
He talks about you in his sleep
And there's nothing I can do to keep
From crying when he calls your name, Jolene
And I can easily understand
You could easily take my man
But you don't know what he means to me, Jolene.

Verse 3
You could have your choice of men
But I could never love again
He's the only one for me, Jolene
I had to have this talk with you
My happiness depends on you
And whatever you decide to do, Jolene.

Streets Of London

Verse 1
Have you seen the old man in the closed down market
Kicking up the papers, with his worn out shoes?
In his eyes you see no pride and held loosely at his side
Yesterday's paper tellin' yesterday's news.

Chorus
So how can you tell me you're lonely
And say for you that the sun don't shine?
Let me take you by the hand and lead you through
    the streets of London
I'll show you something to make you change
    your mind.

Verse 2
Have you seen the old girl who walks the streets
    of London
Dirt in her hair and her clothes in rags?
She's no time for talkin', she just keeps right on walkin'
Carrying her home in two carrier bags.

Verse 3
In the all night cafe at a quarter past eleven
Same old man sitting there on his own
Lookin' at the world over the rim of his tea-cup
Each tea lasts an hour, and he wanders home alone.

Verse 4
Have you seen the old man outside the
    Seaman's Mission?
Memory fading with the medal ribbons that
    he wears
In our winter city, the rain cries a little pity
For one more forgotten hero and a world that
    doesn't care.

Lyrics

Playing

Well done! You've persevered and are now
becoming a versatile player. There are more
advanced things coming up in Part 3, but if you've
understood everything so far, you'll be able to
handle the new ideas.

If you're still making buzzing noises because
your fingers aren't positioned correctly, or if you
still can't change chords smoothly, now is the time
to do something about it. If your strings are in tune
and the notes of the chords ring out clearly, your
performance will sound much better!

Singing

Two things are particularly important for your
singing. Firstly, the pitch of the melody notes
shouldn't be out of your vocal range. Make sure
you can project the lowest notes and don't worry
too much about the highest notes - forcing
them a little will sound fine with modern songs.

Try different capo positions to discover which
key is right for each song. Secondly, breathe
in the natural pauses of a song at the end of lines
or phrases. Don't just breathe anywhere or you
won't be able to put the words over forcefully.

Songs

It's always a great feeling to discover things
yourself and do your own arranging. You've got
plenty of styles and patterns now, so try them out
on new songs that you can find.

Listening

Always listen to what you and others are playing.
The first step is to listen carefully to the notes
when you tune your guitar each day. Then listen to
the sounds you're actually making when you're
playing the songs you know. Finally, listen to
those around you, and of course the professional
guitarists' recording and live performances.
See if you can recognise any of the styles you've
learnt so far!

See you in Part 3 for yet more great songs
and ideas...

Part 3

The Complete Guitar Player

by Russ Shipton
Part 3

Scales

Did you try that bit of homework I gave you at the end of Part 2? Well, if you found it difficult, you'll find the answers to my questions on this page. In a sense, most western music is bound up with the idea of the major scale, so the 'Do Re Mi Fa So La Ti Do' that you've known for some time is more important than you may have thought!

What Is A Scale?

A scale is a series of notes that starts and ends with a note of the same name (but an octave higher). There are various scales, but the major scale, with 8 notes and intervals of: tone, tone, semitone, tone, tone, tone, semitone, is the one which is most important...

The **C** Major Scale

Intervals... **t** = tone   **st** = semi-tone

The Scale And The Melody

You may be wondering what the connection is between the major scale and the songs and accompaniments that you've been singing and playing.

Well, when playing in the key of **C** for example (that usually means starting and ending with a **C** chord), it means that all the melody notes and probably the accompanying notes as well, will normally be from the major scale of the key note, in this case the **C** major scale.

The Scale And Bass Runs

You may have noticed that the common bass runs used in Part 2 are part of the scale. The last half of the scale of **C** is the run you used from the **G** chord to the **C** chord; **g, a, b**, and **c** to finish.

Other Major Scales

Because some chords are a lot easier to finger than others, most guitarists (particularly modern players) will play in the keys of **C, G, D, A,** and **E** (or they might use a capo). The key of **C**, as you see above, has no sharp or flat notes. The others involve one or more notes being sharpened, so that the same intervals exist between the notes. Let's have a look at the **G** major scale...

The **G** Major Scale* (**f** is sharp)

If you look at the gaps or intervals between the notes, you'll notice that only the **f** note must be altered. By making it an **f#**, it is now a whole tone from the **e** note, and a semi-tone to the **g** note.

Now try the **D** Major Scale* (**f** and **c** are sharp)

As with the **G** scale, we have to check the gaps between the notes. For a major scale, they should always be: tone, tone, semi-tone, tone, tone, tone, semi-tone. So the **f** and **c** notes must both be sharpened. Now see if you can work out the notes in the **A** and **E** major scales. All you have to do is to keep the same intervals that the major scale must always have, and flatten or sharpen any notes where necessary.

On the next page we'll look at the relationship of the major scale and chords, but before moving on, practise playing these five scales at the lower end of the fingerboard, and try to remember the notes as you play them.

* The sharp signs (#), at the beginning of a stave, tell you that all those notes, high or low, are always played sharp.

Chords

Now you've got the idea of the major scale, on this page we'll see how the chords you've been using are related to it.

What's A Chord?

A chord is produced when three notes or more are played or held at the same time. These notes are normally found in the major scale of the key that the melody is in, and are either the same as the melody note, or harmonise with it. The chords that you've learnt so far have notes that are always certain intervals apart - intervals that are most natural or pleasing to the ear.

Where Do Chords Come From?

In any particular key, the chords you'd expect to find in an accompaniment come from the major scale of the key or 'tonic' note. Three very important chords are those with their root notes (the note that gives the chord its name) in the 1st, 4th and 5th positions of the scale...

The **C** Major Scale

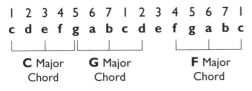

A common major chord consists of three notes: the root note, plus the note two steps above it, plus the note two steps above that one. So the **C** chord (**C** Major chord, in full) has the **c**, **e** and **g** notes in it, while the **F** and **G** chords have **f**, **a** and **c**, and **g**, **b** and **d** notes respectively. One important alternative to the **G** chord is the **G7** chord. This has 4 notes in it: the **g**, **b** and **d** of the **G** chord plus the **f** note.

Apart from the three most important chords shown for the **C** Major Scale, what other chords might you expect in an accompaniment? Well, any of the chords that have their root notes in the other positions of the scale. So, returning to the scale, let's see what chords emerge, if we take two other notes and the root note in the same way as above...

The **C** Major Scale

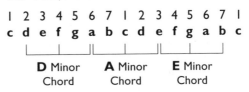

So there are three major chords, **C**, **F** and **G**, plus three minor chords **Dm**, **Em** and **Am**. One more chord, the **B** diminished, would be produced from the **b** (the root note) + the **d** + the **f**, but this diminished chord isn't used as much as the others.

Other Keys

Just as the major scale intervals stay the same, so do the type of chords. Let's have a look at the **G** major scale, and what chords to expect when a song is in the key of **G**...

The **G** Major Scale

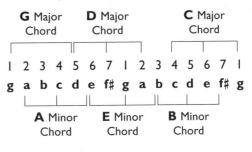

See if you can do the same thing for the keys of **D**, **A**, and **E**.

Chord Variations

So far you've seen slight variations to the usual 3-note major and minor chords. The 7th and minor 7th chords include one more note. You've also played a **sus4** (suspended 4th) chord. Look above and you'll see that the 4th note of the **C** scale is **f**, so to produce a **Csus4** chord, the **f** note is added to the normal **C** major chord, while the **e** note (the 3rd) is taken away.

Chord variations are used more in popular music today, and some are used in the accompaniments for the two Oasis songs in the first section.

Jamaica Farewell

Traditional, arranged by Russ Shipton

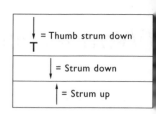

More Syncopation

You're off to the Caribbean for the first song of Part 3! The calypso pattern involves more syncopation, i.e. stress on the offbeat. In fact there are two downstrums on the offbeat and an upstrum on the beat, and the thumb is used to glide across the strings after beat 1. If you prefer to use a flatpick, make the offbeat downstrums shorter than usual.

Accompaniment: 4/4 Rhythm

Melody

The first line uses these notes:

d d d d d e f♯ g
Down the way where the nights are gay

f♯ e d d c c c c b c d
And the sun shines daily on the mountain top.

Notice that all the notes above are from the **G** major scale (shown on page 91), as are the rest of the notes in the song.

Strumming Style

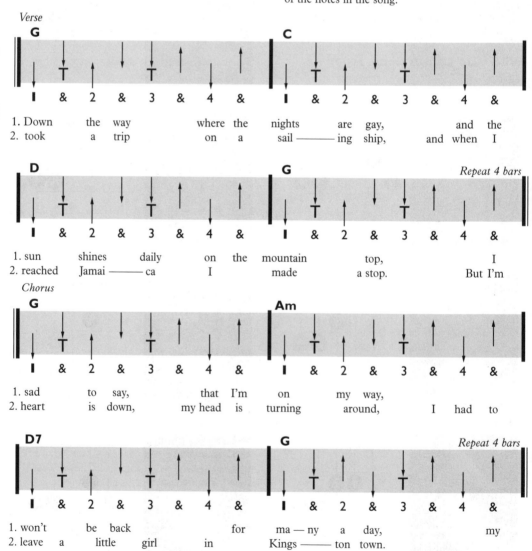

Traditional
© Copyright 2000 Dorsey Brothers Music Limited, 8/9 Frith Street, London W1.
All Rights Reserved. International Copyright Secured.

Wonderwall

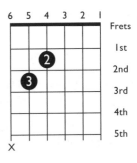

Noel Gallagher

Altered Chords

Guitarists today often use altered chords, where the fingering is unusual or a note (or two) is added to the standard shape. The accompaniment for 'Wonderwall' involves many chords of this kind, three of which have exactly the same name!

Cmaj7 Chord

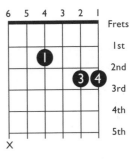

Em7 Chord

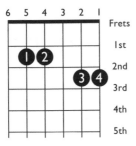

A7sus4(2) **Chord**

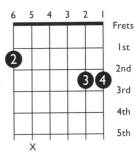

G Chord

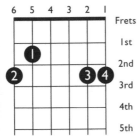

G/F# Chord

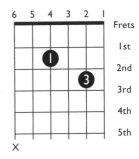

Dsus4 Chord

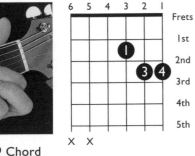

A7sus4(3) **Chord**

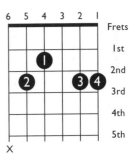

A7sus4(1) **Chord**

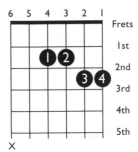

Cadd9 Chord

Strumming Style

93

Wonderwall

Oasis

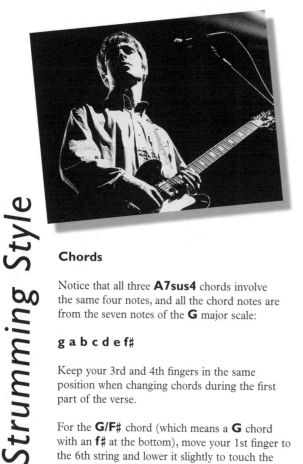

Strumming Style

Chords

Notice that all three **A7sus4** chords involve the same four notes, and all the chord notes are from the seven notes of the **G** major scale:

g a b c d e f♯

Keep your 3rd and 4th fingers in the same position when changing chords during the first part of the verse.

For the **G/F♯** chord (which means a **G** chord with an **f♯** at the bottom), move your 1st finger to the 6th string and lower it slightly to touch the 5th string and stop it vibrating when you strum across the chord.

Rhythm Variations

The main rhythmic feel for this accompaniment is semiquavers, with *downstrums between beats*. As before, make the downstrums on the beats longer and heavier. Some bars have syncopation, with a stress on the semiquaver upstrum before and after beat 3. Make these upstrums longer than usual and do downward airstrokes on beat 3 and halfway between beats 3 and 4.

Sometimes the syncopated stress is only on the upstrum before beat 3, as in the third bar shown (starting with **C maj7**).

General

The speed of this and the next song should be about 90 beats or crotchets per minute, or in standard notation 'andante', which means reasonably slow. If you want to play along with the original recording put your capo on the 2nd fret and play the chord shapes given.

Melody

The first line is shown below. Like the chords in the accompaniment, all the melody notes are from the **G** major scale.

b a g a g a g a a   g   a g
Today is gonna be the day that they're gonna

a g a b g
throw it back to you.

Accompaniment: 4/4 Rhythm

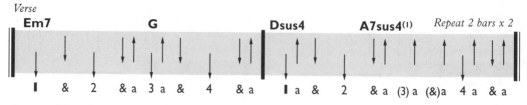

Verse

| **Em7** | **G** | **Dsus4** | **A7sus4**[(1)] | *Repeat 2 bars x 2* |

I & 2 & a 3 a & 4 & a   I a & 2 & a (3) a (&) a 4 a & a

1.   To — day   is gonna be the day that they're gonna throw it back to you.
2.   By now   you should have some-how re-a – lised what you got – ta do.
3. I don't be – lieve that   any   body   feels   the way I do   a – bout you

Wonderwall

Noel Gallagher

Altered Chords

Guitarists today often use altered chords, where the fingering is unusual or a note (or two) is added to the standard shape. The accompaniment for 'Wonderwall' involves many chords of this kind, three of which have exactly the same name!

Cmaj7 Chord

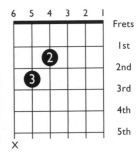

Em7 Chord

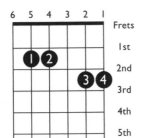

A7sus4[(2)] Chord

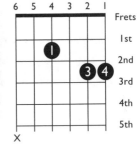

G Chord

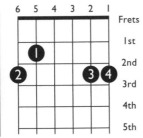

G/F# Chord

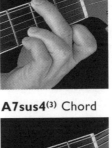
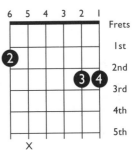

Dsus4 Chord

A7sus4[(3)] Chord

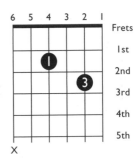

A7sus4[(1)] Chord

Cadd9 Chord

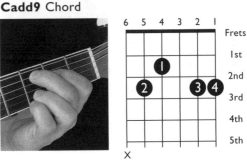

Strumming Style

93

Wonderwall

Oasis

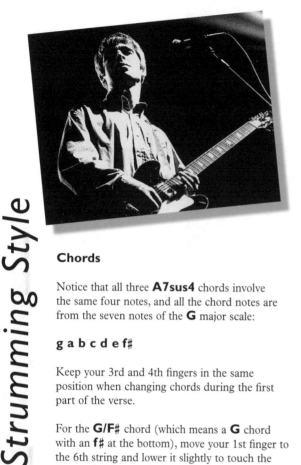

Strumming Style

Chords

Notice that all three **A7sus4** chords involve the same four notes, and all the chord notes are from the seven notes of the **G** major scale:

g a b c d e f♯

Keep your 3rd and 4th fingers in the same position when changing chords during the first part of the verse.

For the **G/F♯** chord (which means a **G** chord with an **f♯** at the bottom), move your 1st finger to the 6th string and lower it slightly to touch the 5th string and stop it vibrating when you strum across the chord.

Rhythm Variations

The main rhythmic feel for this accompaniment is semiquavers, with *downstrums between beats*. As before, make the downstrums on the beats longer and heavier. Some bars have syncopation, with a stress on the semiquaver upstrum before and after beat 3. Make these upstrums longer than usual and do downward airstrokes on beat 3 and halfway between beats 3 and 4.

Sometimes the syncopated stress is only on the upstrum before beat 3, as in the third bar shown (starting with **C maj7**).

General

The speed of this and the next song should be about 90 beats or crotchets per minute, or in standard notation 'andante', which means reasonably slow. If you want to play along with the original recording put your capo on the 2nd fret and play the chord shapes given.

Melody

The first line is shown below. Like the chords in the accompaniment, all the melody notes are from the **G** major scale.

b a g a g a g a a   g   a g
Today is gonna be the day that they're gonna

a g a b g
throw it back to you.

Accompaniment: 4/4 Rhythm

Verse

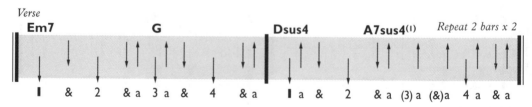

| Em7 | G | Dsus4 | A7sus4(1) | *Repeat 2 bars x 2* |

   1   &   2   &a 3 a &   4   &a   1 a &   2   &a (3) a (&)a 4 a &a

1.   To — day   is gonna be the day that they're gonna throw it back to you.
2.   By   now   you should have some-how re-a – lised what you got – ta do.
3. I don't be – lieve that   any   body   feels   the way I do   a – bout you

	= Strum down
	= Strum up

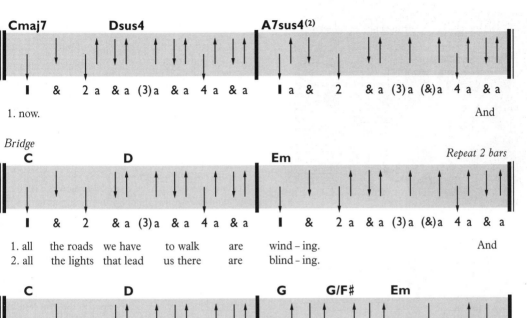

Cmaj7 **Dsus4** **A7sus4**[(2)]

1 & 2 a & a (3)a & a 4 a & a   1 a & 2 & a (3)a (&)a 4 a & a

1. now.   And

Bridge

C **D** **Em**   *Repeat 2 bars*

1 & 2 & a (3)a & a 4 a & a   1 & 2 a & a (3)a (&)a 4 a & a

1. all the roads we have to walk are wind – ing.   And
2. all the lights that lead us there are blind – ing.

C **D** **G** **G/F♯** **Em**

1 & 2 & a (3)a & a 4 a & a   1 a & a 2 a & a 3 & 4 a &

1. There are many things that I would like to say to you, but I don't know

A7sus4[(3)] **A7sus4**[(3)]

1 a & a 2 & 3 a & a (4) a &   1 a & a 2 & 3 a & a (4) a &

1. how,   be-cause

Chorus

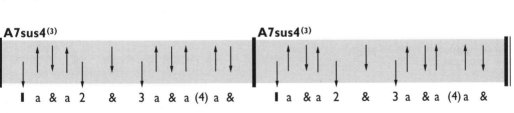

C add 9 **Em7**   **G** **Em**   *Repeat 2 bars x 3*

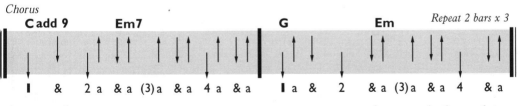

1 & 2 a & a (3)a & a 4 a & a   1 a & 2 & a (3)a & a 4 & a

1. may —— be,   you're gon - na be the one that
2. saves me.   and aft ——— er all,
                  3. you're my wond ———— er - wall.

Words & Music by Noel Gallagher
© Copyright 1995 Oasis Music, Creation Songs Limited & Sony /
ATV Music Publishing (UK) Limited, 10 Great Marlborough Street, London W1.
All Rights Reserved. International Copyright Secured.

Don't Look Back In Anger

Oasis

Chords

Two new chords occur in this arrangement:

Fm6 Chord

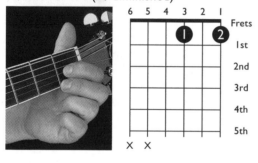

The **Fm6** is similar to the **F** chord but with the 3rd and 4th fingers removed. Both chords include one note that is out of key, i.e. not from the **C** major scale.

Rhythm Patterns

Like the last song, this accompaniment involves semiquavers and downstrums between beats. It should also be played reasonably slowly. There is no syncopation this time, but many slight pattern changes to look out for.

A♭dim Chord (A♭ diminished)

Melody

> **e d d c d c e dca**
> *Slip inside the eye of your mind*

All the melody notes are in key, except the **e♭** for 'take' in the bridge section. The occasional use of out-of-key notes and chords creates a little tension and more interest.

= Strum down

= Strum up

Accompaniment: 4/4 Rhythm

Verse

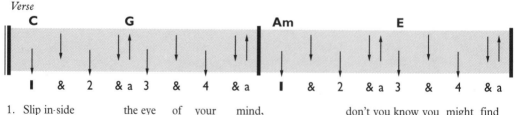

| | & | 2 | & a 3 | & | 4 | & a | | & | 2 | & a 3 | & | 4 | & a |

1. Slip in-side   the eye   of   your   mind,   don't you know you might find
2. You said   that you'd nev — er been,   but all the things that you've seen

Repeat 4 bars

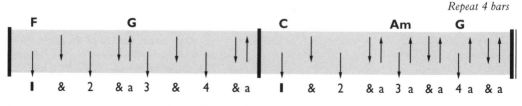

| | & | 2 | & a 3 | & | 4 | & a | | & | 2 | & a 3 a & a | 4 a & a |

1.   a better place to play.
2.   slowly fade a-way.

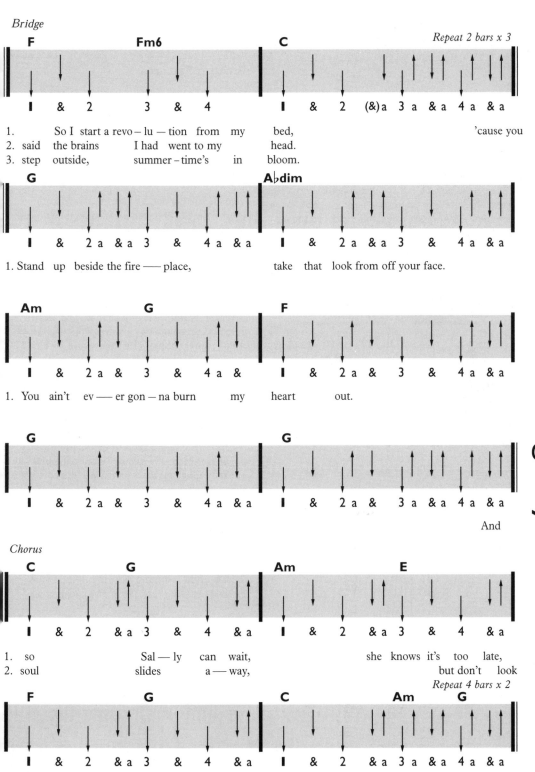

Bridge

F   **Fm6**   **C**   *Repeat 2 bars x 3*

I & 2   3 & 4   I & 2 (&)a 3 a &a 4 a &a

1. So I start a revo – lu — tion from my   bed,   'cause you
2. said the brains   I had went to my   head.
3. step outside,   summer – time's in   bloom.

G   **A♭dim**

I & 2 a &a 3 & 4 a &a   I & 2 a &a 3 & 4 a &a

1. Stand up beside the fire —— place,   take that look from off your face.

Am   **G**   **F**

I & 2 a & 3 & 4 a &   I & 2 a & 3 & 4 a &a

1. You ain't ev —— er gon – na burn   my   heart   out.

G   **G**

I & 2 a & 3 & 4 a &a   I & 2 a & 3 a &a 4 a &a

       And

Chorus

C   **G**   **Am**   **E**

I & 2 & a 3 & 4 & a   I & 2 & a 3 & 4 & a

1. so   Sal — ly can wait,   she knows it's too late,
2. soul   slides   a — way,   but don't look

Repeat 4 bars x 2

F   **G**   **C**   **Am**   **G**

I & 2 & a 3 & 4 & a   I & 2 &a 3 a &a 4 a &a

1.   as we're walk – ing on by.   Her
2. back in an — ger,   I heard you say.

Strumming Style

Words & Music by Noel Gallagher

Copyright 1995 Oasis Music, Creation Songs Limited & Sony /
/ Music Publishing (UK) Limited, 10 Great Marlborough Street, London W1.
ghts Reserved. International Copyright Secured.

Lay Down Sally

Eric Clapton

Boogies

The boogie is a special type of rhythmic accompaniment which normally involves adding a '6th' note to the chord on the 2nd and 4th beats. This note is called a 6th because it is six steps above the chord root note (see page 91). The strums are much shorter than usual and the chord shapes are not standard. This is the simplest way that the **A**, **D** and **E** chords can be held for playing 'Lay Down Sally':

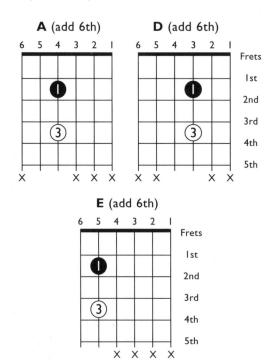

A (add 6th) **D (add 6th)**

E (add 6th)

Accompaniment: 4/4 Rhythm

Rhythm Patterns

Just two strings are played for each chord, so both downstrums and upstrums are short. Add the 6th note on the 2nd beat of each bar and then remove it immediately. Add the 6th again on the 4th beat. Remove it again before you play the 1st beat of the next bar.

Two alternating patterns are given, and both involve the 6th note being added on the 2nd and 4th beats. Keep the flatpick (or fingers) near the strings and only move the right hand a little.

Damping

A very important technique for playing 'heavier' guitar accompaniments involves stopping strings from ringing on after clear notes have been sounded. This can be done by the left hand fingers releasing the pressure on the strings but still keeping contact with them.

When you've mastered the boogie patterns given for 'Lay Down Sally', try damping the 6th note that is added on the 2nd and 4th beats. Add the 3rd finger, do the strum and then release the pressure but keep touching the string. Make the note last just short of half a beat.

Melody

This song has a blues feel to it, which explains the use of the natural **g** note in the scale of **A** major. Here's the first line of lyrics with notes:

g   g   g a   b b   a
There is nothing that is wrong

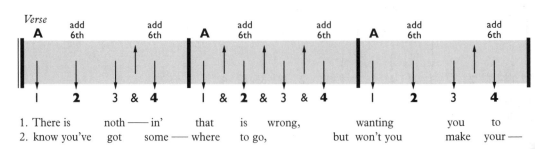

Verse

1. There is   noth —— in'   that   is   wrong,   wanting   you   to
2. know you've   got   some —— where   to go,   but won't you   make   your —

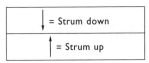

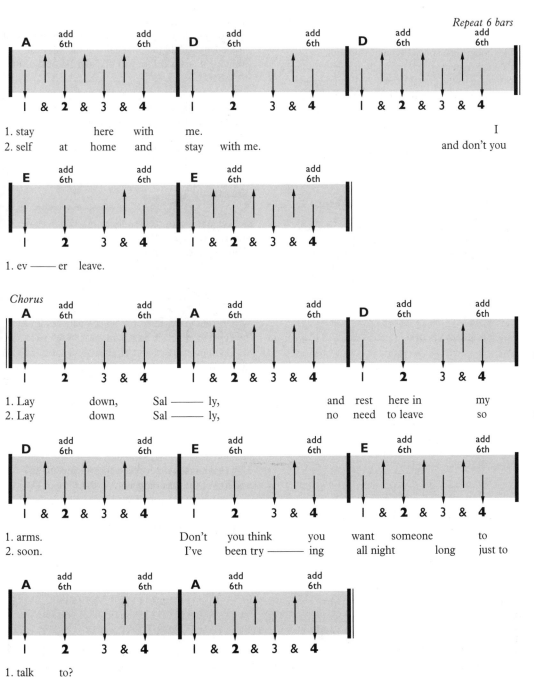

rds & Music by Eric Clapton, Marcy Levy & George Terry
Copyright 1977 & 1999 Eric Clapton (33.33%) & Throat Music/
ner Chappell Music Limited, Griffin House, 161 Hammersmith Road, London W6 (66.67%).
All rights Reserved. International Copyright Secured.

Can't Buy Me Love

The Beatles

Bass-Strum Style

Swing Bass-Strum

You've already used the swing rhythm in the strumming style. Some bass-strum songs also need to be swung, and as before, the upstrums between beats are delayed (as indicated visually) to produce a jumpy feel.

New Chord Shapes

'Can't Buy Me Love' has a blues feel, and that means **7**th chords can be used instead of the normal major chords:

G7 Chord

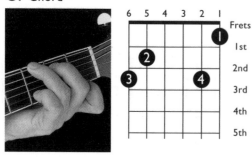

6	5	4	3	2	1	
					❶	Frets
		❷				1st
❸				❹		2nd
						3rd
						4th
						5th

C7 Chord

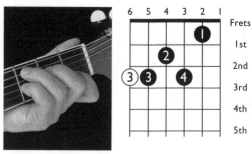

6	5	4	3	2	1	
				❶		Frets
			❷			1st
❸	❸		❹			2nd
						3rd
						4th
						5th

D7 Chord

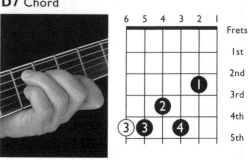

6	5	4	3	2	1	
						Frets
						1st
				❶		2nd
		❷				3rd
❸	❸		❹			4th
						5th

This **G7** version includes the **d** note on the 2nd string held by the 4th finger. The **C7** shape is moved up two frets to produce this **D7** version.

If you strum across the open 1st string, that will create a **D9** chord. This 9th chord has five notes, including the 7th and 9th notes, **c** and **e**. The 3rd finger can be moved to the 6th string for the **C7** and **D7** chords, as shown.

Rhythm Pattern

One pattern is shown throughout but try making some changes to the number of upstrums and which bass string is struck. Repeat the twelve verse bars for Verse 2 before going to the chorus. Stop playing on the 1st beat of the last bar, sing 'Can't buy me' and then start the **Bm** bar.

For the **Bm** chord in this arrangement, you need to do a 'full' barre across all 6 strings.

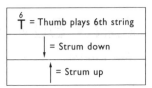

Accompaniment: 4/4 Swing Rhythm

Verse

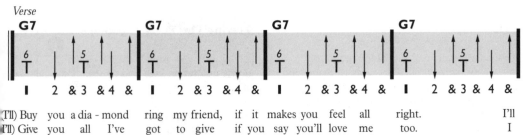

(I'll) Buy you a dia - mond   ring my friend,   if it makes you   feel   all   right.   I'll
(I'll) Give you   all   I've   got   to give   if you   say you'll love   me   too.   I

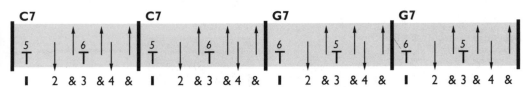

1. get   you   an — y ——— thing my friend,   if it makes you   feel   all   right.   'Cause
2. may   not have a   lot   to   give but what I've got   I'll   give to   you.

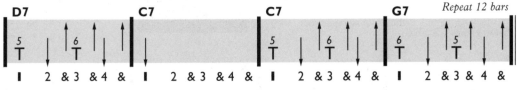

Repeat 12 bars

1. I   don't   care   too   much for money,   money can't buy me   love.
2. I   don't   care   too   much for money,   money can't buy me   love.   2. Can't   buy me

Chorus

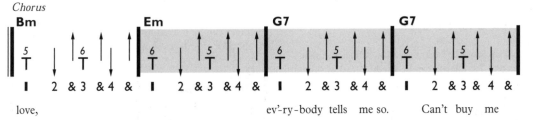

love,   ev'-ry-body tells   me so.   Can't buy   me

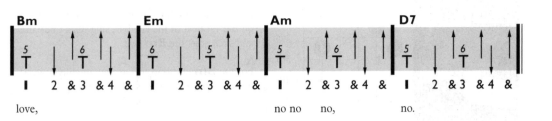

love,   no no   no,   no.

Words & Music by John Lennon & Paul McCartney

She'll Be Coming Round The Mountain

Traditional, arranged by Russ Shipton

Two Parts

Now I have something special for you to try:
to learn two parts with different chord shapes and
play one along with the other. The first part is
the accompaniment in the key of **A** major with
the **A**, **D** & **E** chords. For the second part, where
the melody is picked out, *a capo is placed at the
second fret* and the **G**, **C** & **D7** shapes are played.

Playing The Parts Together

Those of you working in the classroom can
divide into two groups, and those at home can play
along with a friend or a tape recorder.

First learn this simple accompaniment for
a well-known traditional American song, which
includes hammer-ons and runs...

Bass-Strum Style

Accompaniment: 4/4 Rhythm

Verse

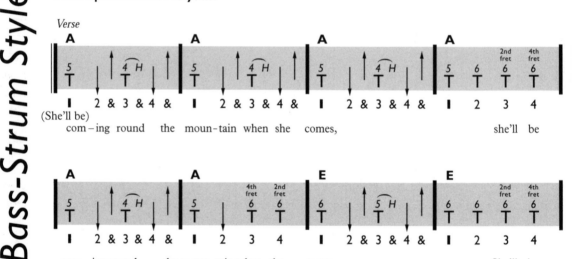

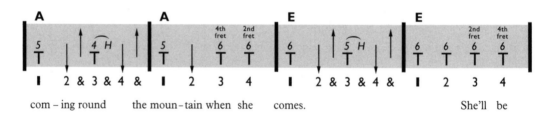

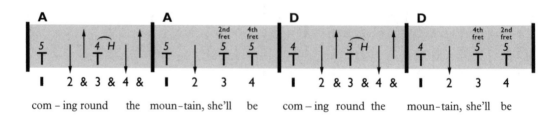

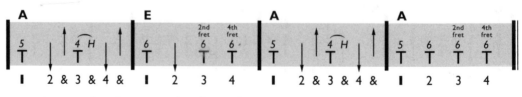

$\frac{5}{T}$	= Thumb plays 5th string
↓	= Strum down
↑	= Strum up

Picking Out The Melody

Go through this arrangement carefully. Hold the usual chords, but move the most convenient finger to play the melody notes that aren't in the shape you're holding. These are indicated by string and fret numbers. Picking out the tune means striking treble strings more than usual. The strums should be kept short.

In bar 3, hammer the 1st finger onto the 2nd fret 3rd string for the **a** note. In bar 6 the 3rd finger is moved to the 2nd string 3rd fret for the **d** note,

and can be left there for the following down/up strums. The top string is left open. Finally the 3rd finger is removed for an open 2nd string **b** note.

In the 8th and 12th bars, use your 4th finger for the **d** and **g** notes respectively. The **D7** bar near the end involves a bass run to **G**. Bring your 1st finger up for the **f♯**. Use your 1st finger for the two hammer-ons in the penultimate bar.

Solo: Capo 2nd fret G = A D7 = E7 C = D

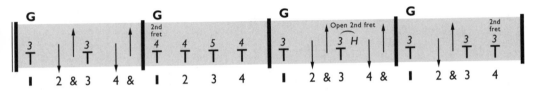

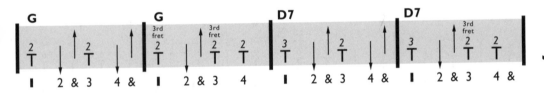

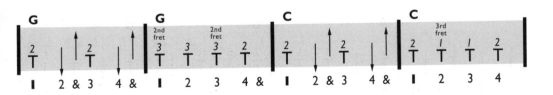

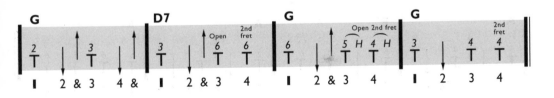

Traditional
© Copyright 2000 Dorsey Brothers Music Limited, 8/9 Frith Street, London W1.
All Rights Reserved. International Copyright Secured.

Suzanne

Leonard Cohen

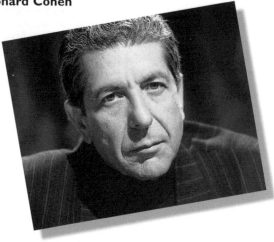

Syncopated Arpeggio

The pattern for this great Leonard Cohen song includes one thumb strike between beats. This offbeat stress suits ballads like 'Suzanne'. The middle strings are used to match the atmosphere of this haunting and intense song.

Watch for varied bass notes and quick hammer-ons. Move the 2nd finger to the 5th string for the **b** note of the slow bass run from **C** to **G** in bar 16.

Pinches

A two string pinch, where bass and treble strings are played at the same time, is also used in the arpeggio style. Use your thumb and 3rd finger (for the top string) at the start of five chorus bars.

D7/F♯ Chord

The **D7/F♯** chord (**D7** with **f♯** as bass) is another slightly altered chord that many guitarists use, especially in the key of **G** major. Hold the usual **D7** shape and bring the thumb over for the **F♯** on the 2nd fret of the 6th string.

Melody

The melody notes as well as chords are all in key except for an occasional **f** natural. Here is the first line of the melody:

d d d d e d d d d d d e d
Suzanne takes you down to her place by the river

Accompaniment: 4/4 Rhythm

Verse

1. (Su-)zanne   takes you   down,   to her place   near   the river,   you can
2. when you mean   to tell her,   that you have   no love   to give her,   then she

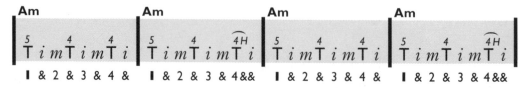

1. hear   the boats   go   by,   you can spend   the night   be — side her,   and you
2. gets you   on   her wavelength,   and she lets   the river   answer,   that you've

104

Arpeggio Style

G	G	G	G
6 4 4	6 5 4	6 4 4	6 5 4
T *i* *m* T *i* *m* T *i*	T *i* *m* T *i* *m* T *i*	T *i* *m* T *i* *m* T *i*	T *i* *m* T *i* *m* T *i*
1 & 2 & 3 & 4 &	1 & 2 & 3 & 4 &	1 & 2 & 3 & 4 &	1 & 2 & 3 & 4 &

1. know that she's half crazy, but that's why you want to be there, and she
2. always been her lover.
And you
(to Chorus)

Bm	Bm	C	C — *Repeat first 12 bars*
5 4 4	5 4 4	5 4 4	5 (2nd fret) 5 (Open) 5
T *i* *m* T *i* *m* T *i*	T *i* *m* T *i* *m* T *i*	T *i* *m* T *i* *m* T *i*	T *i* *m* T *i* *m* T *i*
1 & 2 & 3 & 4 &	1 & 2 & 3 & 4 &	1 & 2 & 3 & 4 &	1 & 2 & 3 & 4 &

1. feeds you tea and oranges that come all the way from China. And just
(to start)

Chorus

Bm	Bm	C	C
5 4 4	5 4 4	5 4 4	5 (2nd fret) 5 (Open) 5
P *i* *m* T *i* *m* T *i*	P *i* *m* T *i* *m* T *i*	P *i* *m* T *i* *m* T *i*	T *i* *m* T *i* *m* T *i*
1 & 2 & 3 & 4 &	1 & 2 & 3 & 4 &	1 & 2 & 3 & 4 &	1 & 2 & 3 & 4 &

1. want to travel with her, and you want to travel blind, and you

G	G	Am	D7/F#
6 4 4	6 4 4	5 4 4	6 (2nd fret) 4 5
T *i* *m* T *i* *m* T *i*	T *i* *m* T *i* *m* T *i*	T *i* *m* T *i* *m* T *i*	T *i* *m* T *i* *m* T *i*
1 & 2 & 3 & 4 &	1 & 2 & 3 & 4 &	1 & 2 & 3 & 4 &	1 & 2 & 3 & 4 &

1. know that she will trust you, for you've touched her perfect body with your

G	G
6 4 4	6 4 4
P *i* *m* T *i* *m* T *i*	P *i* *m* T *i* *m* T *i*
1 & 2 & 3 & 4 &	1 & 2 & 3 & 4 &

1. mind.

Going Places

Russ Shipton

Swing Arpeggio

The rhythm can be swung in all styles, and here's a swing arpeggio instrumental. Delay the notes between beats until just before the following beat. (The sign before the notation indicates that the beat note should be twice as long as the second note between beats).

This and the next piece are in standard notation to give you more practice at reading notes. Hold the chords indicated and you'll find the notes quickly.

Out-Of-Key Notes

This piece has a blues feel, so the **g** natural (not in the key scale of **E** major) sounds fine. It also makes changing chords easier! In bar 3 take your hand off the **E** chord and use your 1st finger for the **a♯**, which runs to **b**. Use your 3rd finger for the low **g** natural note in bars 5 and 6, again with your hand off the chord.

In bar 8 move your 2nd finger from the 5th to 6th string. Bars 9 and 10 involve more flattened, bluesy notes and the out-of-key chords **E7** and **Am**. You could use your 2nd, 3rd and 4th fingers for the **A** to make the change to **Am** easier.

Use the 1st finger for the **g** natural to **g♯** hammer-on in the last bar.

Arpeggio Style

Music by Russ Shipton
© Copyright 2000 Dorsey Brothers Music Limited, 8/9 Frith Street, London W1.
All Rights Reserved. International Copyright Secured.

Off The Wall

Russ Shipton

The Pull-Off

Another common embellishment is the 'pull-off', which in a sense is the opposite of the hammer-on. A fretted note is sounded by the right hand playing a string, then a second note is produced by the left hand finger coming off the string to an open string or a lower fret note.

The word 'pull' is used because the finger must pull or bend the string slightly (towards the ground) before lifting off. This ensures the second note will be loud enough.

Hold the 2nd fret of the 1st string with your 1st or 2nd finger. Sound the **f♯** note then pull the string slightly towards the ground and release the string to produce an open **e**.

General

Here's another opportunity for you to play in the 6/8 rhythm. Remember that the main stresses are on the 1st and 4th beats. This is made easier to read in standard notation because the two sets of three quavers are joined together.

Use the thumb for the bass strings and three fingers for the trebles, as usual.

Use the normal chord shapes and fingering. In the **D** chord bars the 2nd fret is pulled off to the open 1st string. Put the 2nd finger back when you need to play the **f♯**. In the **A** bars the 3rd finger is pulled off from the 2nd fret to the open 2nd string. The **E** bars mean pulling the 4th finger off from the 3rd fret to the open 2nd string.

Arpeggio Style

Accompaniment: 6/8 Rhythm

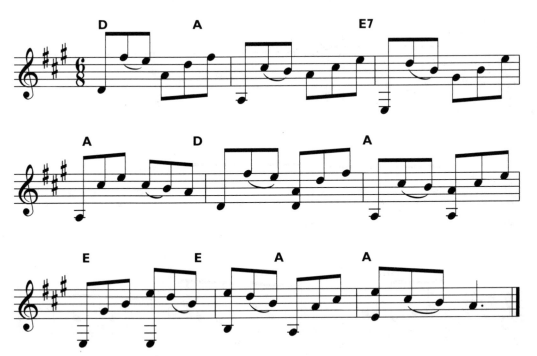

Music by Russ Shipton

Always On My Mind

Willie Nelson

Arpeggio Style

This imitates the Willie Nelson recording, and is a short run to the **C** chord. For this pinch only, strike the 2nd string with your middle finger.

The last bar involves two quick chord changes on beats 3 and 4. This produces a strong and interesting 'push' back to the start of the next verse.

Chords

All the chords are fingered as usual for this accompaniment, apart from **Dm/C**. This requires a different fingering for the **Dm** chord. The 4th finger is placed on the 2nd string so the 3rd finger can hold the **c** note:

Dm/C Chord

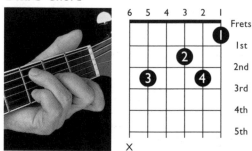

Melody

All the melody notes are in key, though the **D** chord is used for variety. Here is the first line:

e f g f e   e   d   c   d e d d c   b   a
Maybe I didn't treat you quite as good as I should hav

More Pattern Variations

The arrangement for this well-known ballad, made famous by both Willie Nelson and Elvis Presley, includes different kinds of syncopation, pinches, hammer-ons and a variety of bass runs. Go over each bar carefully.

Bar 1 of the lead-in has an offbeat thumb strike between beats 1 and 2. Bars 2 and 6 of the verse also include this syncopation. Notice the quick chord change on the last beat in bar 4 of the verse.

Accompaniment: 4/4 Rhythm

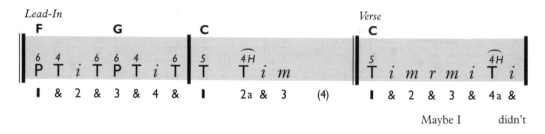

P = Pinch thumb & Ring finger

T = Thumb

i = Index finger

m = Middle finger

r = Ring finger

Arpeggio Style

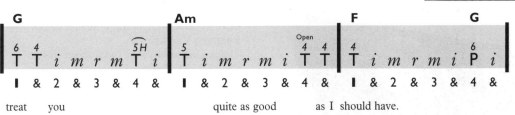

treat you   quite as good   as I should have.

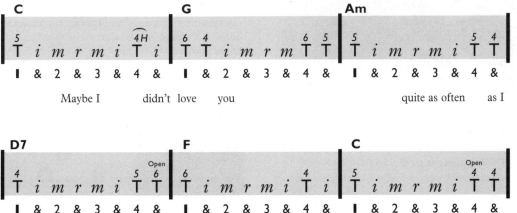

Maybe I   didn't love   you   quite as often   as I

could have.   If I made you feel   second best,

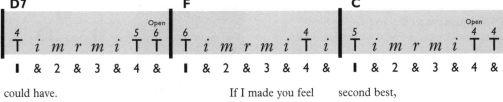

girl, I'm sorry   I was   blind.   You were al-ways on my

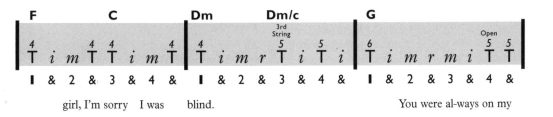

mind,   you were al-ways on my mind.

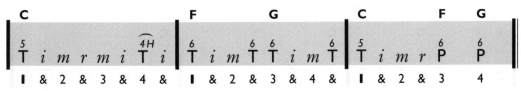

Words & Music by Wayne Thompson, Mark James & Johnny Christopher
© Copyright 1971 (renewed 1979) Screen Gems-EMI Music Incorporated & Rose Bridge Music Incorporated, USA.
Screen Gems-EMI Music Limited, 127 Charing Cross Road, London WC2 (75%) & Chelsea Music Publishing Company Limited, 124 Great Portland Street, London W1 (25%).
All Rights Reserved. International Copyright Secured.

Imagine

John Lennon

Arpeggio Style

Slow Arpeggio

The arpeggio patterns you've played so far have been mid-tempo to fast. For some slower patterns, each beat is stressed more and plucks of more than one string can be used to fill out the sound:

4/4 Rhythm Finger **G**

	6 T	*i*	*r* *m*	*i*	*r* *m*	*i*	*r* *m*	*i*
	I	&	2	&	3	&	4	&

For the 3/4 rhythm remove the notes in the last beat. My arrangement of 'Imagine' includes ideas from the original, but to imitate John Lennon's piano style you could experiment with this kind of pattern. The chord comes on the beat with a pluck of three fingers, with the bass notes struck by the thumb between beats:

Accompaniment: 4/4 Rhythm

4/4 Rhythm Finger **C**

r *m* *i*	5 T	*r* *m* *i*	5 T	*r* *m* *i*	5 T	*r* *m* *i*	5 T
I	&	2	&	3	&	4	&

Pattern Variations

The lead-in includes ideas from the original recording. Move your 3rd finger for the **f♯** on the 4th fret of the 4th string. This is followed by the 2nd fret of the 4th string to begin the **C** bar, instead of the root note.

The end of this bar has a fast **e f f♯** run on the 4th string. Use your 2nd, 3rd and 4th fingers. You could try a hammer-on from the **e** to **f**.

The 3rd bar then begins with the open **d** instead of the root note. A slow, downward bass run comes at the end of the verse, beginning with **c** and ending on **f♯**. Raise your 2nd finger to the 5th string for the **b** and bring your 4th finger over for the **Am/G** chord. Use your thumb for the 6th string **f♯** note of **D/F♯**.

The middle section adds another bass note to the pattern occasionally. Use your 1st finger for the **a♯** leading to **B7**. The final bar imitates the original recording with a run on the 6th string from **e** to **f** to **f♯**. The **g** at the start of the next verse completes the run.

Melody

All the melody notes are in key, though the **B7** chord is used as a passing chord to add interest to the middle section. Here's the first line:

d d d d f♯ f♯ e d d d d f♯ f♯ e

Imagine there's no heaven, it's easy if you try

Lead-In

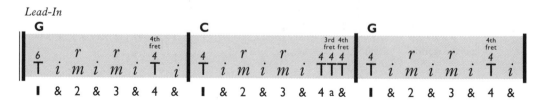

| T = Thumb |
| *i* = Index finger |
| *m* = Middle finger |
| *r* = Ring finger |

Arpeggio Style

Verse

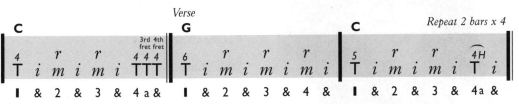

I–mag-ine there's no hea-ven
it's eas–y if you try
no hell be–low us
a-bove us only sky.

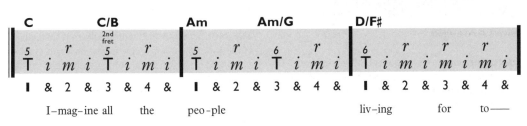

I–mag-ine all the peo-ple liv–ing for to——

Chorus

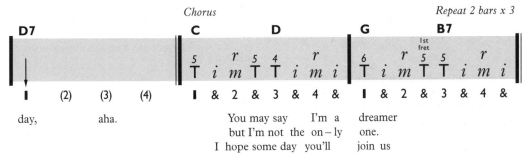

day, aha.

You may say I'm a dreamer
but I'm not the on–ly one.
I hope some day you'll join us

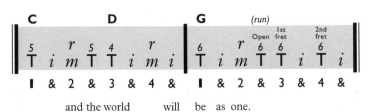

and the world will be as one.

Words & Music by John Lennon

111

Don't Think Twice, It's All Right

Bob Dylan

Alternating Thumb Style

For the hammer-ons in the **Bm**, **A7** and **E7** bars, the 1st finger of the left hand hammers down from the open *2nd string* to the usual fret for the chord.

Bass Runs

Bass runs in alternating thumb patterns are similar to those in the bass-strum style. There are three runs given in the accompaniment. The first from **A7** to **D** (**b c♯ d**), the second from **D7** to **G** (**e f♯ g**), and the last from **G** to **E** (**g f♯ e**).

Use the appropriate fingers for the run notes, and leave the other fingers in position as long as possible.

General

Bob Dylan plays this piece extremely fast. 'Prestissimo' as classical musicians would say, which means over 200 beats per minute! When you've done a lot of practice, put your capo on the 2nd fret and play along with the original recording.

Hammer-ons

In the alternating thumb style a hammer-on often involves a treble string and a pinch:

D

4

P H

I &

The lower curved line means the hammer-on will be on the *treble* string. The 2nd finger is off its usual position in the **D** chord, and hammers down after the pinch. The thumb plays the 4th string and the middle finger the 1st string.

Melody

To make sure you start singing the song in the same key you're playing, here are the notes for the first line:

f♯ f♯   f♯ f♯   f♯ a a   a f♯   d   b
It ain't no use   to sit and wonder why babe

Accompaniment: 4/4 Rhythm

D	A	Bm	Bm
4⌒ 3 4 3	5 3 5 3	5 3 5 3	5⌒ 3 5 3
P H T i T m T	T i T m T i T	T T i T m T	P H T m T i T
I & 2 & 3 & 4	I & 2 & 3 & 4	I 2 & 3 & 4	I & 2 & 3 & 4

1. (It)ain't no   use   to   sit   and won – der   why   babe,
2. ain't no   use   to   sit   and won – der   why   babe,

112

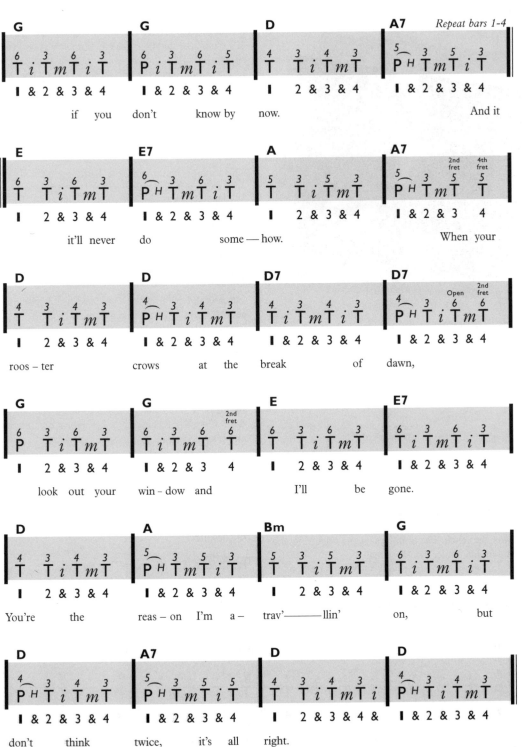

Words & Music by Bob Dylan
© Copyright 1963 Warner Brothers Music, USA. © Copyright renewed 1990 SPECIAL RIDER MUSIC.
This arrangement © Copyright 2000 SPECIAL RIDER MUSIC.
All Rights Reserved. International Copyright Secured.

The Boxer

Paul Simon

Use the right hand fingers in the same way as for the arpeggio style. The index finger strikes the 3rd string, the middle strikes the 2nd string, and the ring finger strikes the 1st string. Play the pattern over and over using the correct fingers, then try inventing some variations of your own before having a go at 'The Boxer'.

Pattern Variations

This arrangement is similar to Paul Simon's original recording, though one or two extra bars of **C** have been omitted. Also, the second verse, not the 1st verse, leads to the chorus. Notice the first bar of **C** where a pinch comes on the 2nd beat and your 3rd finger moves to the 6th string on the 3rd beat. You've already played the run from **C** to **Am** which comes in the 3rd bar.

Check each bar of the accompaniment carefully because there are many slight pattern changes. For variety and more dynamics when playing solo, the bass strum style can be used for the chorus. You then return to alternating thumb patterns for the following verse.

Three Treble Strings

Using three right hand fingers for alternating patterns gives more variety. Try this pattern:

Melody

All the chords and melody notes are in key. Here is the first line:

g g g a g e e f g g c b a
I am just a poor boy though my story's seldom told

4/4 Rhythm Hold **G**

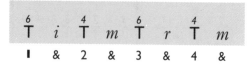

Accompaniment: 4/4 Rhythm

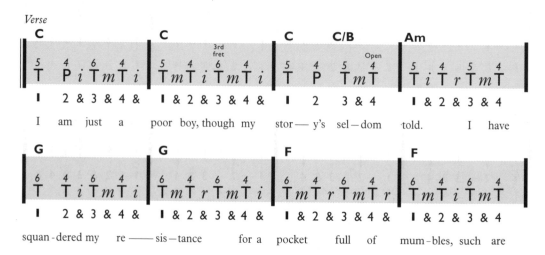

Alternating Thumb Style

114

P	=	Pinch thumb & Ring finger
T	=	Thumb
i	=	Index finger
m	=	Middle finger
r	=	Ring finger

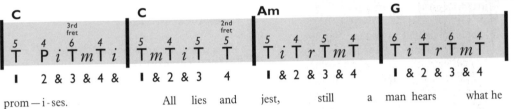

C (3rd fret)
5 T 4 P 6 i T m 4 T i
1 2 & 3 & 4 &

prom — i - ses.

C (2nd fret)
5 T m 4 T i 5 T T 5 T
1 & 2 & 3 4

All   lies   and

Am
5 T i 4 T r 5 T m 4 T
1 & 2 & 3 & 4

jest,   still   a   man hears   what he

G
6 T i 4 T r 6 T m 4 T
1 & 2 & 3 & 4

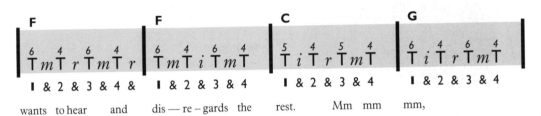

F
6 T m 4 T r 6 T m 4 T r
1 & 2 & 3 & 4 &

wants to hear   and

F
6 T m 4 T i 6 T m 4 T
1 & 2 & 3 & 4

dis — re – gards the   rest.

C
5 T i 4 T r 5 T m 4 T
1 & 2 & 3 & 4

Mm mm   mm,

G
6 T i 4 T r 6 T m 4 T
1 & 2 & 3 & 4

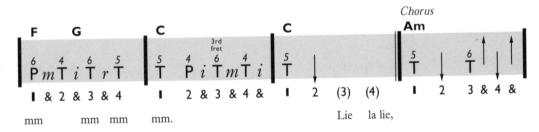

F   G
6 P m 4 T i 6 T r 5 T
1 & 2 & 3 & 4

mm   mm mm   mm.

C (3rd fret)
5 T P 4 i T 6 m T 4 i
1 2 & 3 & 4 &

C
5 T ↓
1 2 (3) (4)

Lie   la lie,

Chorus
Am
5 T ↓ 6 T ↑ ↓
1 2 3 & 4 &

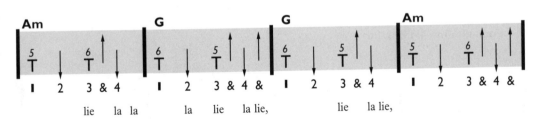

Am
5 T ↓ 6 T ↑ ↓
1 2 3 & 4

lie   la la

G
6 T ↓ 5 T ↑ ↓
1 2 3 & 4 &

la lie   la lie,

G
6 T ↓ 5 T ↑ ↓
1 2 3 & 4

lie   la lie,

Am
5 T ↓ 6 T ↑ ↓
1 2 3 & 4 &

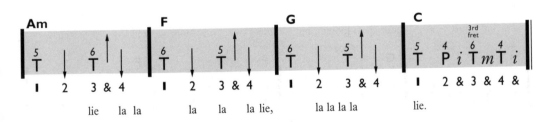

Am
5 T ↓ 6 T ↑ ↓
1 2 3 & 4

lie   la la

F
6 T ↓ 5 T ↑ ↓
1 2 3 & 4

la la la lie,

G
6 T ↓ 5 T ↑ ↓
1 2 3 & 4

la la la la

C (3rd fret)
5 T 4 P i 6 T m 4 T i
1 2 & 3 & 4 &

lie.

Words & Music by Paul Simon
© Copyright 1968 Paul Simon.
All Rights Reserved. International Copyright Secured.

The 59th Street Bridge Song (Feelin' Groovy)

Paul Simon

Alternating Thumb Style

Swing Alternating Thumb

Most swing alternating thumb accompaniments are found in blues and ragtime music, but not all. This Paul Simon song has a swing rhythm, and as before the notes between beats are delayed. Again, in my notation this is shown visually.

G/B Chord

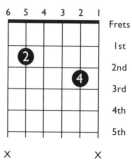

Pattern Variations

Three right hand fingers should be used for this arrangement. When a pinch is indicated, pluck the 1st string with your ring finger except for the **G/B** chord where you strike the 2nd. Notice the syncopation in all the bars except 2 and 5. Move quickly to the **G/B** or **G** chord just before the 3rd beat.

Melody

All the notes and chords are in key for this song. Here is the first line:

e   d   b   c   d   b
Slow down, you move too fast

Accompaniment: 4/4 Swing Rhythm

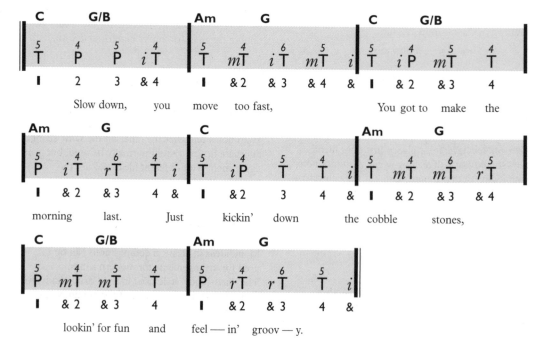

More Ideas

Classical compositions aren't as pattern-like as the modern styles you've been learning. Partly because they stand on their own as instrumentals and need variations from bar to bar and section to section, and partly because they don't involve the normal heavy beat stress of popular music.

So far you've tried just one classical piece, and that was a simple, one-note-at-a-time arrangement. On these next pages there are some intermediate level compositions which explore some more ideas of the classical guitar style.

Follow the information on this page and the notes given before each piece and you shouldn't find them too difficult. Take them very slowly at first.

Rest Signs

As well as signs for note length, there need to be signs for different times of pause, or silence. The note signs were given in Part 2.

Here are the rest signs:

    = **Quaver rest**

    = **Crotchet rest**

    = **Minim rest**

    = **Semi-breve rest**

Dotted Notes

When notes have a dot placed just after them, they should last half as long again. A minim note with a dot (dotted minim) lasts for the equivalent of three crotchets or 3 beats in 3/4 and 4/4. A dotted crotchet lasts for three quavers or one and a half beats in 3/4 or 4/4.

2/4 Rhythm

Classical music often involves rhythms other than 3/4 and 4/4. When a piece is written in 2/4, the '2' means two beats, and the '4' means each beat is a crotchet in length. So the two stress points are on the first and second crotchets.

Key Signatures

By checking the key signatures at the start of each line of music, you know which notes to play sharp and you can work out the key of the piece. The piece by Carulli ends on a **c** note and has no sharps indicated at the start of each line. This means the key is **C** major.

'Call And Answer' ends with a **G** chord and has one sharp indicated. This means it is written in the key of **G** major. 'Passing Note Waltz' ends on a **d** and has two sharps shown. This means it is written in the key of **D** major.

Try to remember the number of sharps for each key. This will help in understanding and playing all types of music.

Left Hand Fingering

Classical players generally use only the left hand fingers they need at any one time. So in these pieces you can forget about holding whole chord shapes. Work out which fingers are strictly necessary and use only those. Economical use of fingers makes for smoother playing.

Sometimes there may be a choice of finger to use. Experiment with different possibilities and choose the one that you're comfortable with.

Right Hand Fingering

One set of possibilities for right hand fingering is given above the notation for each piece. With notes one after the other on the same string, alternate fingers should normally be used, but again, experiment with different ideas and use the fingering that's best for you.

Applications

Many ideas in classical compositions can be used for arrangements for modern songs. The 'bass-pluck' style used in the Carulli study, for example, can be used successfully in humorous or story-type songs.

Study

Fernando Carulli

Rhythm

This study was written by Fernando Carulli
about 170 years ago. Because it's in the 3/4 rhythm,
there are three beats per bar and each beat is the
equivalent of a crotchet in length.

Key

No sharp (or flat) signs at the start of each
line means the piece is in the key of **C** major or
A minor. Because the last note is **c**, this means
the key is **C** major. The last 'chord' is **C**, but try to
work out which is the underlying chord for the
other bars.

Classical Style

Instrumental: 3/4 Rhythm

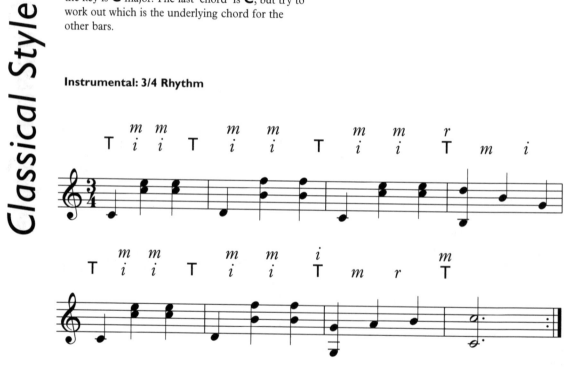

Left Hand Fingering

You can use the 1st and 3rd fingers in the 4th bar,
or the 2nd and 4th. In the 7th bar the 2nd finger
can be used for the low **g** note, with the 1st playing
the **a** note that follows. Or you could use the 3rd
and 2nd fingers.

Passing Note Waltz

Russ Shipton

T	= Thumb
i	= Index finger
m	= Middle finger
r	= Ring finger

Two Part Notation

The last piece was written as one part, but really
the music involves two distinct parts: the treble
(melody) and the bass (rhythm and harmony).

In this piece I've separated bass and treble parts by
using note stems that go down and up respectively.
You'll see that each part must add up to three
crotchets of time (three beats here) for each bar.
Work out the timing of each part, then put them
together.

Instrumental: 3/4 Rhythm
Standard Musical Notation

Key

What major scale has two sharp notes?
Check the last note as well and you'll work out the
key very quickly. Try to discover the underlying
chords for each bar.

If you played the piece using full chord shapes,
try playing it again using only the fingers actually
needed.

Passing Notes

The treble passing notes (run notes) are easy
to find. Raise a finger that's down or add another.
In the 3rd and 6th bars, for example, you can add
your 3rd finger for the **d** note on the 2nd string.

Call And Answer

Russ Shipton

T = Thumb	
i = Index finger	
m = Middle finger	
r = Ring finger	

General

As the title suggests, this piece involves a switch from a treble to a bass line, and back again - a sort of question and answer arrangement that is used sometimes in Indian music, pop and blues, and also in opera. In the first bar let the bass ring on for the whole duration (two beats), while in the second bar make sure the treble note rings for the full bar.

Key

The sharp sign at the start of each line of notation means you're in the key of **G** major. There are two 'accidentals' (called such because they are not in the major scale of **G**) in the 6th and 7th bars, so they have a sharp sign before them. The other sign, in the 2nd, 4th, 10th and 12th bars, is called a 'natural' and simply means that you ignore the key signature wherever you see one.

Instrumental: 2/4 Rhythm

Classical Style

(Strum)

Music by Russ Shipton

Jamaica Farewell

Verse 1
Down the way where the nights are gay
And the sun shines daily on the mountain top
I took a trip on a sailing ship
And when I reached Jamaica I made a stop.

Chorus
But I'm sad to say that I'm on my way
Won't be back for many a day
My heart is down, my head is turning around
I had to leave a little girl in Kingston Town.

Verse 2
Down in the market you can hear
Ladies cry out as on their heads they bear
"Akai rice, salt fish are nice"
And the rum is fine any time of year.

Verse 3
Sounds of laughter everywhere
And the dancing girls swing to and fro'
I must declare my heart is there
Though I've been from Maine to Mexico.

Wonderwall

Verse 1
Today is gonna be the day that they're gonna throw
    it back to you
By now you should have somehow realised what
    you gotta do
I don't believe that anybody feels the way I do about
    you now.

Verse 2
Back beat, the word is on the street that the fire in
    your heart is out
I'm sure you've heard it all before, but you never
    really had a doubt
I don't believe that anybody feels the way I do
    Em7 G Dsus4 A7sus4
    about you now.

Bridge 1
And all the roads we have to walk are winding
And all the lights that lead us there are blinding
There are many things that I would like to say to
    you but I don't know how.

Chorus
Because maybe, you're gonna be the one that saves me
And after all, you're my wonderwall.

Verse 3
Today was gonna be the day but they'll never
    throw it back to you
By now you should've somehow realised what you're
    not to do
I don't believe that anybody feels the way I do
    about you now.

Bridge 2
And all the roads that lead you there were winding
And all the lights that light the way are blinding
There are many things that I would like to say to you
But I don't know how.

Don't Look Back In Anger

Verse 1
Slip inside the eye of your mind
Don't you know you might find a better place to play
You said that you'd never been
But all the things that you've seen slowly fade away

Bridge 1
So I start a revolution from my bed
'Cause you said the brains I had went to my head
Step outside, Summertime's in bloom
Stand up beside the fireplace
Take that look from off your face
You ain't ever gonna burn my heart out.

Chorus
And so Sally can wait, she knows it's too late
As we're walking on by
Her soul slides away, "But don't look back in anger"
I heard you say.

Verse 2
Take me to the place where you go
Where nobody knows if it's night or day
But please don't put your life in the hands
Of a rock 'n' roll band who'll throw it all away.

Bridge 2
I'm gonna start a revolution from my bed
'Cause you said the brains I had went to my head
Step outside, 'cause Summertime's in bloom
Stand up beside the fireplace
Take that look from off your face
'Cause you ain't ever gonna burn my heart out.

Chorus 2
And so Sally can wait, she knows it's too late
As she's walking on by
My soul slides away, 'But don't look back in anger'
I heard you say.

Lay Down Sally

Verse 1
There is nothing that is wrong in wanting you to
    stay here with me
I know you've got somewhere to go, but won't you
    make yourself at home and stay with me?
And don't you ever leave.

Chorus
Lay down Sally, and rest here in my arms
Don't you think you want someone to talk to?
Lay down Sally, no need to leave so soon
I've been trying all night long just to talk to you.

Verse 2
The sun ain't nearly on the rise and we still got
    the moon and stars above
Underneath the velvet skies, love is all that matters
    won't you stay with me?
And don't you ever leave.

Verse 3
I long to see the morning light, colouring your
    face so dreamily
So don't you go and say goodbye, you can lay your
    worries down and stay with me
And don't you ever leave.

Can't Buy Me Love

Intro
Bm Em Bm Em
Can't buy me lo — ve,   lo — ve
Am D7
Can't buy me lo — ve.

Verse 1
I'll buy you a diamond ring, my friend
If it makes you feel all right
I'll get you anything, my friend
If it makes you feel all right
'Cause I don't care too much for money
Money can't buy me love.

Verse 2
I'll give you all I've got to give
If you say you love me too
I may not have a lot to give
But what I've got I'll give to you
I don't care too much for money
Money can't buy me love.

Chorus
Can't buy me love, everybody tells me so
Can't buy me love, no no no, no.

Verse 3
Say you don't need no diamond rings
And I'll be satisfied
Tell me that you want the kind of things
That money just can't buy
I don't care too much for money
Money can't buy me love.

Bm Em Bm Em
Can't buy me lo — ve,   lo — ve
Am D7 G7
Can't buy me lo — ve.

Lyrics

Lyrics

She'll Be Coming Round The Mountain

Verse 1
She'll be coming round the mountain when·
    she comes (x2)
She'll be coming round the mountain (x2)
She'll be coming round the mountain when she comes.

Verse 2
She'll be driving six white horses when she comes (x2)
She'll be driving six white horses (x2)
She'll be driving six white horses when she comes.

Verse 3
She'll be wearing pink pyjamas when she comes (x2)
She'll be wearing pink pyjamas (x2)
She'll be wearing pink pyjamas when she comes.

Verse 4
She will have to sleep with Grandma when
    she comes (x2)
She will have to sleep with Grandma (x2)
She will have to sleep with Grandma when she comes.

Verse 5
And we'll all go to meet her when she comes (x2)
And we'll all go to meet her (x2)
Oh we'll all go to meet her when she comes.

Suzanne

Verse 1
Suzanne takes you down to her place near the river
You can hear the boats go by, you can spend the
    night beside her
And you know that she's half crazy, but that's why
    you want to be there
And she feeds you tea and oranges that come all the
    way from China
And just when you mean to tell her that you have no
    love to give her
She gets you on her wavelength and she lets the
    river answer
That you've always been her lover.

Chorus
And you want to travel with her
And you want to travel blind
And you know that she will trust you
For you've touched her perfect body with your mind.

Verse 2
And Jesus was a sailor when he walked upon the water
And he spent a long time watching from his lonely
    wooden tower
And when he knew for certain only drowning men
    could see him
He said "All men will be sailors then until the sea
    shall free them"
But he himself was broken long before the sky
    would open
Foresaken, almost human, he sank beneath your
    wisdom like a stone.

Chorus 2
And you want to travel with him
And you want to travel blind
And you think maybe you'll trust him
For he's touched your perfect body with his mind.

Verse 3

Now Suzanne takes your hand and she leads you to
    the river
She is wearing rags and feathers from Salvation
    Army counters
And the sun pours down like honey on our lady of
    the harbour
And she shows you where to look among the garbage
    and the flowers
There are heroes in the seaweed, there are children in
    the morning
They are leaning out for love, and they will lean that
    way forever
While Suzanne holds the mirror.

Chorus 3

And you want to travel with her
And you want to travel blind
And you know that you can trust her
For she's touched your perfect body with her mind.

Always On My Mind

Verse 1

Maybe I didn't treat you
Quite as good as I should have
Maybe I didn't love you
Quite as often as I could have
Little things I should have said and done
I just never took the time
You were always on my mind
You were always on my mind.

Verse 2

Maybe I didn't hold you
All those lonely, lonely times
And I guess I never told you
I'm so happy that you're mine
If I made you feel second best
Girl I'm so sorry I was blind
You were always on my mind
You were always on my mind.

Middle Section

 C Am F   **Dm**
Tell me, tell me that your sweet love hasn't died
 C Am   **F**
Give me give me one more chance
            G   **C**
   to keep you satisfied satisfied.

Imagine

Verse 1

Imagine there's no heaven
It's easy if you try
No hell below us
Above us only sky
Imagine all the people living for today, aha..

Verse 2

Imagine there's no countries
It isn't hard to do
Nothing to kill or die for
And no religion too
Imagine all the people living life in peace, aha..

Chorus

You may say I'm a dreamer
But I'm not the only one
I hope some day you'll join us
And the world will be as one.

Verse 3

Imagine no possessions
I wonder if you can
No need for greed or hunger
A brotherhood of man
Imagine all the people, sharing all the world, aha..

Lyrics

Don't Think Twice, It's All Right

Verse 1
It ain't no use to sit and wonder why babe
If you don't know by now
And it ain't no use to sit and wonder why, babe
It'll never do somehow
When your rooster crows at the break of dawn
Look out your window and I'll be gone
You're the reason I'm a-travellin' on
But don't think twice, it's all right.

Verse 2
It ain't no use in turnin' on your light babe
The light I never knowed
And it ain't no use in turnin' on your light babe
I'm on the dark side of the road
But I wish there was something you would do or say
To try and make me change my mind and stay
But we never did too much talkin' anyway
But don't think twice, it's all right.

Verse 3
So it ain't no use in callin' out my name gal
Like you never done before
And it ain't no use in callin' out my name gal
I can't hear you anymore
I'm a-thinkin' and a-wonderin' walkin' down the road
I once loved a woman, a child I'm told
I give her my heart but she wanted my soul
But don't think twice, it's all right.

Verse 4
So long honey babe
Where I'm bound, I can't tell
But goodbye's too good a word babe
So I'll just say "Fare thee well"
I ain't a-sayin' you treated me unkind
You could have done better but I don't mind
You just kinda wasted my precious time
But don't think twice, it's all right.

The Boxer

Verse 1
I am just a poor boy, though my story's seldom told
I have squandered my resistance for a pocketful of
    mumbles, such are promises
All lies and jest, still a man hears what he wants to hear
    and disregards the rest.

Verse 2
When I left my home and my family, I was no more
    than a boy
In the company of strangers, in the quiet of a railway
    station, running scared
Laying low, seeking out the poorer quarters where the
    ragged people go
Looking for the places only they would know.

Chorus
Lie la lie, lie la la la la lie la lie
Lie la lie, lie la la la la la la lie la la la la lie.

Verse 3
Asking only workman's wages, I come looking for a job
But I get no offers, just a come-on from the whores on
    Seventh Avenue
I do declare there were times when I was so lonesome,
    I took some comfort there
Ooh la la, la la la la.

Verse 4
Then I'm laying out my winter clothes and wishing
    I was gone
Going home, where the New York City winters aren't
    C   **C C**
bleeding me,
         Em Am   **G G C C**
Leading me,   going home.

Verse 5
In the clearing stands a boxer and a fighter by his trade
And he carries the reminders of every glove that laid
    him down
Or cut him till he cried out in his anger and his shame
"I am leaving, I am leaving" but the fighter still
    remains.

The 59th Street Bridge Song
(Feelin' Groovy)

Verse 1
Slow down, you move too fast
You've got to make the morning last
Just kicking down the cobble stones
Lookin' for fun and feelin' groovy.

Verse 2
Hello lamppost, watcha knowin'?
I've come to watch your flowers growin'
Ain'tcha got no rhymes for me?
Dootin' doo-doo, feelin' groovy.

Verse 3
I got no deeds to do, no promises to keep
I'm dappled and drowsy and ready to sleep
Let the morning time drop all its petals on me
Life, I love you, all is groovy.

Lyrics

Closing Comments

Congratulations!

You've worked successfully through all three parts of *The Complete Guitar Player* course and are now a competent and versatile guitarist. You've mastered patterns and techniques in four distinct and popular right hand styles which you can use to play a wide variety of rock, pop, folk and country songs. You've also had a useful introduction to the classical style and music theory.

But don't stop here, of course. There's a wealth of material out there that you can start playing right now. To progress further with your guitar playing, why not check out the supplementary books in *The Complete Guitar Player* series, including the Tablature Book, and a huge range of songbooks including many popular songs.

See the complete Music Sales catalogue for full details of these and many other great guitar books (details on page 4).

I hope that you have enjoyed this course and will continue to learn and play the guitar.

Good luck!

1/06(57583)